TEACHER'S PET PUBLICATIONS

LITPLAN TEACHER PACK
for
A Separate Peace
based on the book by
John Knowles

Written by
Mary B. Collins

© 1996 Teacher's Pet Publications
All Rights Reserved

This **LitPlan** for John Knowles'
A Separate Peace
has been brought to you by Teacher's Pet Publications, Inc.

Copyright Teacher's Pet Publications 1996
11504 Hammock Point
Berlin MD 21811

Only the student materials in this unit plan
such as worksheets, study questions, assignment sheets, and tests
may be reproduced multiple times for use in the purchaser's classroom.

For any additional copyright questions,
contact Teacher's Pet Publications.

www.tpet.com

TABLE OF CONTENTS - *A Separate Peace*

Introduction	5
Unit Objectives	7
Reading Assignment Sheet	8
Unit Outline	9
Study Questions (Short Answer)	13
Quiz/Study Questions (Multiple Choice)	20
Pre-reading Vocabulary Worksheets	35
Lesson One (Introductory Lesson)	49
Nonfiction Assignment Sheet	52
Oral Reading Evaluation Form	54
Writing Assignment 1	57
Writing Assignment 2	62
Writing Assignment 3	69
Writing Evaluation Form	60
Vocabulary Review Activities	63
Extra Writing Assignments/Discussion ?s	66
Unit Review Activities	81
Unit Tests	85
Unit Resource Materials	113
Vocabulary Resource Materials	127

A FEW NOTES ABOUT THE AUTHOR
JOHN KNOWLES

KNOWLES, JOHN. John Knowles was born in Fairmont, West Virginia. He received his education from Philips Exeter Academy and Yale University. Mr. Knowles started his writing career as a newspaper reporter and later became an associate editor of *Holiday*.

In addition to *A Separate Peace*, John Knowles has written a number of other novels, including *Morning in Antibes, Indian Summer, Double Vision,* and *Peace Breaks Out.* He also has published a collection of short stories entitled *Phineas*.

His writing has won many awards, including the William Faulkner Foundation Award, the Rosenthal Award of the National Institute of Arts and Letters, and an award from the Independent School Education Board.

INTRODUCTION

This unit has been designed to develop students' reading, writing, thinking, and language skills through exercises and activities related to *A Separate Peace* by John Knowles. It includes twenty lessons, supported by extra resource materials.

The **introductory lesson** introduces students to the first class project relating to this unit. Following the introductory activity, students are given a transition to explain how the activity relates to the book they are about to read. Following the transition, students are given the materials they will be using during the unit. At the end of the lesson, students begin the pre-reading work for the first reading assignment.

The **reading assignments** are approximately thirty pages each; some are a little shorter while others are a little longer. Students have approximately 15 minutes of pre-reading work to do prior to each reading assignment. This pre-reading work involves reviewing the study questions for the assignment and doing some vocabulary work for 8 to 10 vocabulary words they will encounter in their reading.

The **study guide questions** are fact-based questions; students can find the answers to these questions right in the text. These questions come in two formats: short answer or multiple choice. The best use of these materials is probably to use the short answer version of the questions as study guides for students (since answers will be more complete), and to use the multiple choice version for occasional quizzes. If your school has the appropriate equipment, it might be a good idea to make transparencies of your answer keys for the overhead projector.

The **vocabulary work** is intended to enrich students' vocabularies as well as to aid in the students' understanding of the book. Prior to each reading assignment, students will complete a two-part worksheet for approximately 8 to 10 vocabulary words in the upcoming reading assignment. Part I focuses on students' use of general knowledge and contextual clues by giving the sentence in which the word appears in the text. Students are then to write down what they think the words mean based on the words' usage. Part II nails down the definitions of the words by giving students dictionary definitions of the words and having students match the words to the correct definitions based on the words' contextual usage. Students should then have an understanding of the words when they meet them in the text.

After each reading assignment, students will go back and formulate answers for the study guide questions. Discussion of these questions serves as a **review** of the most important events and ideas presented in the reading assignments.

After students complete reading the work, there is a **vocabulary review** lesson which pulls together all of the fragmented vocabulary lists for the reading assignments and gives students a review of all of the words they have studied.

Following the vocabulary review, a lesson is devoted to the **extra discussion questions/writing assignments**. These questions focus on interpretation, critical analysis and personal response, employing a variety of thinking skills and adding to the students' understanding of the novel.

The **group activity** which follows the discussion questions has students working in small groups to discuss the main themes of the novel. Using the information they have acquired so far through individual work and class discussions, students get together to further examine the text and to brainstorm ideas relating to the themes of the novel.

The group activity is followed by a **reports and discussion** session in which the groups share their ideas about the themes with the entire class; thus, the entire class is exposed to information about all of the themes and the entire class can discuss each theme based on the nucleus of information brought forth by each of the groups.

There are three **writing assignments** in this unit, each with the purpose of informing, persuading, or having students express personal opinions. The first assignment is to inform: students relate one event from the book as a hard news story. The second assignment is to express personal opinions: students write an editorial. The third assignment is to persuade: students create an advertisement for their newspapers.

In addition, there is a **nonfiction reading assignment**. Students are required to read one newspaper article from a local newspaper during each week of the unit, a total of four articles.

The **review lesson** pulls together all of the aspects of the unit. The teacher is given four or five choices of activities or games to use which all serve the same basic function of reviewing all of the information presented in the unit.

The **unit test** comes in two formats: short answer and multiple choice. As a convenience, two different tests for each format have been included. In addition, there is an advanced short answer unit test for higher level students.

There are additional **support materials** included with this unit. The **extra activities section** includes suggestions for an in-class library, crossword and word search puzzles related to the novel, and extra vocabulary worksheets. There is a list of **bulletin board ideas** which gives the teacher suggestions for bulletin boards to go along with this unit. In addition, there is a list of **extra class activities** the teacher could choose from to enhance the unit or as a substitution for an exercise the teacher might feel is inappropriate for his/her class. **Answer keys** are located directly after the **reproducible student materials** throughout the unit. The student materials may be reproduced for use in the teacher's classroom without infringement of copyrights. No other portion of this unit may be reproduced without the written consent of Teacher's Pet Publications, Inc.

UNIT OBJECTIVES *A Separate Peace*

1. While reading John Knowles's *A Separate Peace,* students will consider the effects of war and the intricacies of friendships.

2. Students will demonstrate their understanding of the text on four levels: factual, interpretive, critical, and personal.

3. Students will create a newspaper relating to the events in the story.

4. Students will plan and execute an "American Spirit" day for the whole school.

5. Students will see that each of our daily life experiences changes us and shapes our thoughts and feelings.

6. Students will be given the opportunity to practice reading aloud and silently to improve their skills in each area.

7. Students will answer questions to demonstrate their knowledge and understanding of the main events and characters in *A Separate Peace* as they relate to the author's theme development.

8. Students will enrich their vocabularies and improve their understanding of the novel through the vocabulary lessons prepared for use in conjunction with the novel.

9. The writing assignments in this unit are geared to several purposes:
    a. To have students demonstrate their abilities to inform, to persuade, or to express their own personal ideas
       NOTE: Students will demonstrate ability to write effectively to <u>inform</u> by developing and organizing facts to convey information. Students will demonstrate the ability to write effectively to <u>persuade</u> by selecting and organizing relevant information, establishing an argumentative purpose, and by designing an appropriate strategy for an identified audience. Students will demonstrate the ability to write effectively to <u>express personal ideas</u> by selecting a form and its appropriate elements.
    b. To check the students' reading comprehension
    c. To make students think about the ideas presented by the novel
    d. To encourage logical thinking
    e. To provide an opportunity to practice good grammar and improve students' use of the English language.

READING ASSIGNMENT SHEET - *A Separate Peace*

Date Assigned	Chapters Assigned	Completion Date
	1-3	
	4-5	
	6-7	
	8-9	
	10-13	

UNIT OUTLINE - *A Separate Peace*

1 Introduction PV 1-3	2 Read 1-3 PV 4-5	3 Study ?s 1-3 Read 4-5 PV 6-7	4 Study ?s 4-5 Read 6-7	5 Writing Assignment #1
6 Study ?s 6-7 PVR 8-9	7 Study ?s 8-9 PVR 10-13	8 Study ?s 10-13 Group Activity Writing Conferences	9 Writing Assignment #2	10 Vocabulary
11 Group Activity	12 Reports & Discussion	13 Extra ?s	14 Writing Assignment #3	15 Newspaper Working Session
16 Introduce Class Project	17 Class Project Working Session	18 Library/Resource	19 Review	20 Test

Key: P = Preview Study Questions   V = Prereading Vocabulary Work   R = Read

STUDY GUIDE QUESTIONS

SHORT ANSWER STUDY GUIDE QUESTIONS - *A Separate Peace*

Chapters 1 - 3
1. What two sites did the narrator go back to see at Devon?
2. Who is Phineas?
3. What unusual thing did Phineas talk Gene into doing?
4. Why were the boys not punished for jumping out of the tree?
5. Identify Mr. Prud-homme and Mr. Patch-Withers.
6. What was the Super Suicide Society of the Summer Session?
7. Gene said, "I didn't need to feel any tremendous rush of gratitude towards Phineas." Why not?
8. Why did Gene continue jumping out of the tree and going along with Phineas even though he didn't want to?
9. What was blitzball?
10. In what way does Gene describe his memories of the war years?
11. What does the swimming record incident show about Phineas?
12. "Exposing a sincere emotion like that at the Devon School was the next thing to suicide." What had Phineas just told Gene?

Chapters 4-5
1. What two realizations does Gene have about his relationship with Phineas?
2. Over what did Gene and Phineas argue?
3. What happened to Phineas?
4. Why didn't Gene tell Phineas the truth (that he bounced on the limb and caused the fall) at the infirmary?
5. What is Phineas' reaction when Gene does confess?

Chapters 6-7
1. "If you broke the rules, then they broke you." What did Gene mean?
2. Identify Cliff Quackenbush.
3. How did Gene lose his job of Assistant Crew Manager?
4. From whom was Gene's long-distance call?
5. Why did Gene feel a sense of freedom when Phineas said, "Listen, pal, if I can't play sports, you're going to play them for me"?
6. What idea does Brinker Hadley introduce?
7. Why did Gene leave the Butt Room without smoking a cigarette?
8. What "good deed" did the boys do?
9. What does Gene say about Brinker as he tries to spare Leper's feelings when the gang meets him after the railroad work is done?
10. Who decided to enlist?
11. Why did Gene not enlist?

A Separate Peace Short Answer Study Guide Page 2

Chapters 8-9
1. Of what did Finny try to convince Gene about the war?
2. For what event did Finny want to train Gene? What was wrong with that plan?
3. Why did Phineas decide that Mr. Ludsbury didn't know the war was just propaganda from fat old men?
4. Who was the first of Gene's gang to actually enlist?
5. What effect did Leper's enlistment have on the boys at Devon?
6. What winter event did Phineas invent?
7. From whom was Gene's telegram, and what was the message?

Chapters 10-11
1. What happened to Leper?
2. How did Gene react to Leper's description of what happened to him?
3. Why did Gene want to see only Phineas?
4. Brinker said, "What's the matter with our class anyway? It isn't even June yet and we've already got two men sidelined for the Duration." Who was he talking about? For the duration of what?
5. How did Leper's illness affect Phineas?
6. Contrast Brinker's view of Finny's disability with Gene's view.
7. Where did Brinker take Gene and Finny? Why?
8. Why did Finny rush out of the room?
9. What happened to Finny after he ran out of the room?

Chapters 12-13
1. Why didn't Gene do anything to help with Phineas after his second accident?
2. Why did Gene sneak into the infirmary?
3. Gene told Phineas, "you wouldn't be any good in the war, even if nothing had happened to your leg." What did he mean?
4. What finally happened to Phineas?
5. What was ironic about Gene's part in the war?

ANSWER KEY: STUDY GUIDE QUESTIONS - *A Separate Peace*

Chapters 1 - 3

1. What two sites did the narrator go back to see at Devon?
    He came to see the First Academy Building and the tree.

2. Who is Phineas?
    He is the narrator's (Gene's) best friend and roommate.

3. What unusual thing did Phineas talk Gene into doing?
    He talked him into jumping from the limb of a tall tree into the river, an activity which was dangerous at best.

4. Why were the boys not punished for jumping out of the tree?
    It was summertime and wartime, and the school masters were a little more lenient than usual with the boys. Mostly, though, Finny had a gift of gab--a manner of speaking which made people like him and overlook his faults and transgressions.

5. Identify Mr. Prud-homme and Mr. Patch-Withers.
    Mr. Prud-homme was a substitute master for the summer. Mr. Patch-Withers was the stern, summer Head Master.

6. What was the Super Suicide Society of the Summer Session?
    Gene and Finny and their friends formed this group to formalize the jumping out of the tree ritual.

7. Gene said, "I didn't need to feel any tremendous rush of gratitude towards Phineas." Why not?
    Although Finny had offered his hand and "saved" Gene when Gene lost his balance, Gene figured he wouldn't have been there in the first place if Finny hadn't talked him into it.

8. Why did Gene continue jumping out of the tree and going along with Phineas even though he didn't want to?
    "Otherwise I would have lost face with Phineas, and that would have been unthinkable."

9. What was blitzball?
    It was a game Phineas made up in which the odds were against the ball carrier and all the players are "enemies."

10. In what way does Gene describe his memories of the war years?
    He gives the characteristics of America during that time (as he remembered them).

11. What does the swimming record incident show about Phineas?
    He has nothing to prove to anyone else--only himself. He wants to break the record for himself and for fun, not for the recognition or glory.

12. "Exposing a sincere emotion like that at the Devon School was the next thing to suicide." What had Phineas just told Gene?
    Phineas had just told Gene that Gene was his best pal.

Chapters 4-5
1. What two realizations does Gene have about his relationship with Phineas?
    A. Phineas was jealous of Gene's being head of the class.
    B. Phineas had deliberately set out to wreck Gene's studies.

2. Over what did Gene and Phineas argue?
    They argued over whether or not Gene should study or go watch Leper Lepellier jump from the tree. At first Gene said he needed to study and that Leper wouldn't jump anyway. Phineas agreed that it would be okay if Gene wouldn't go. Then Gene immediately felt as if he had to go (and he did).

3. What happened to Phineas?
    Gene bounced on the limb he and Phineas were standing on in the tree. Phineas fell and badly broke his leg. His sports career was ended.

4. Why didn't Gene tell Phineas the truth (that he bounced on the limb and caused the fall) at the infirmary?
    Phineas had told him he just fell (even though he thought maybe Gene had jumped on the limb). Before Gene could confess, Dr. Stanpole came in.

5. What is Phineas' reaction when Gene does confess?
    He doesn't want to believe it. When he realized that it was true, he just wanted Gene to leave. They parted on fairly friendly terms.

Chapters 6-7
1. "If you broke the rules, then they broke you." What did Gene mean?
    The boys in the summer session were not supposed to be jumping from the tree; it was against the rules. Gene figured that the tragedy with Phineas was their payment for breaking the rules.

2. Identify Cliff Quackenbush.
    He was the crew manager of the rowing team. He was a physically mature student and was rude to those he considered beneath himself (most people).

3. How did Gene lose his job of Assistant Crew Manager?
   He got in a fight with Quackenbush and hit him. Both ended up in the river.

4. From whom was Gene's long-distance call?
   The call was from Finny.

5. Why did Gene feel a sense of freedom when Phineas said, "Listen, pal, if I can't play sports, you're going to play them for me"?
   He feels forgiven by Phineas and given a way to make up for his meanness--and he feels he and Finny would be even closer friends from this point forward: ". . . this must have been my purpose from the start: to become a part of Phineas."

6. What idea does Brinker Hadley introduce?
   He said that Gene bounced Finny out of the tree on purpose.

7. Why did Gene leave the Butt Room without smoking a cigarette?
   The boys in the Butt Room, led by Brinker Hadley, tease Gene and insinuate more strongly that they know (or think) that he is responsible for Phineas' accident. Gene is so shaken that he wishes only to escape, to leave. Using French studies as an excuse, he exits.

8. What "good deed" did the boys do?
   They cleared the railroad tracks of snow so the troop trains could go through.

9. What does Gene say about Brinker as he tries to spare Leper's feelings when the gang meets him after the railroad work is done?
   He says that Brinker "couldn't be put off with half a story."

10. Who decided to enlist?
    Brinker and Gene decided to enlist.

11. Why did Gene not enlist?
    Phineas returned.

Chapters 8-9

1. Of what did Finny try to convince Gene about the war?
   He tried to convince him that there was no war; fat old men made it up so they would have all the best while the rest of the country suffered.

2. For what event did Finny want to train Gene? What was wrong with that plan?
   He wanted to train him for the 1944 Olympics. The Olympics had been canceled because of the war.

3. Why did Phineas decide that Mr. Ludsbury didn't know the war was just propaganda from fat old men?
   Mr. Ludsbury was thin.

4. Who was the first of Gene's gang to actually enlist?
   Leper Lepellier was the first to enlist.

5. What effect did Leper's enlistment have on the boys at Devon?
   "This established our liaison with World War II."

6. What winter event did Phineas invent?
   He invented the Winter Carnival.

7. From whom was Gene's telegram, and what was the message?
   It was from Leper. It said, "I have escaped and need help. . . ."

Chapters 10-11
1. What happened to Leper?
   He went AWOL because he was about to get a Section Eight discharge (a discharge for mentally ill soldiers).

2. How did Gene react to Leper's description of what happened to him?
   Gene told Leper to shut up. He didn't want to hear it. It didn't have anything to do with him. He ran away and left Leper alone.

3. Why did Gene want to see only Phineas?
   Only Phineas was removed from the war--a safe harbour for Gene.

4. Brinker said, "What's the matter with our class anyway? It isn't even June yet and we've already got two men sidelined for the Duration." Who was he talking about? For the duration of what?
   He was talking about Phineas and Leper and their inability to go fight for the duration of the war, school, life.

5. How did Leper's illness affect Phineas?
   It made the war real, inescapable. He could no longer pretend there was no war. He realized that he would not be a part of it. He realized that he would not be a part of any physical contest.

6. Contrast Brinker's view of Finny's disability with Gene's view.
   Brinker thought the boys should tease Finny to help him face his disability and get on with his life. Gene thought the boys should ignore it, be silent, in hopes that it would get better.

7. Where did Brinker take Gene and Finny? Why?
>He took them to the First Building. He had a group of students who were to investigate Finny's accident to determine Gene's guilt or innocence. Brinker wanted all of the facts out in the open so everything about the accident would be resolved prior to graduation.

8. Why did Finny rush out of the room?
>He didn't want to face the facts. He knew that Gene was responsible, but he wanted to ignore that fact.

9. What happened to Finny after he ran out of the room?
>He fell down the marble stairs and broke his leg again.

Chapters 12-13

1. Why didn't Gene do anything to help with Phineas after his second accident?
>He again felt responsible. He felt Finny would only get more upset by seeing him. He was in a thought-filled daze.

2. Why did Gene sneak into the infirmary?
>He wanted to apologize to Phineas.

3. Gene told Phineas, "You wouldn't be any good in the war, even if nothing had happened to your leg." What did he mean?
>Phineas was the kind of a person who might jump across enemy lines at night to pay a social call. By being so friendly with everyone and having his gift of gab, the whole war would become a mess--people wouldn't be able to tell the enemy from friends, generals would get confused by his explanations, etc. Phineas' basic nature was not one conducive to being a soldier.

4. What finally happened to Phineas?
>He died. Bone marrow got into his blood stream and stopped his heart.

5. What was ironic about Gene's part in the war?
>After all that concern about the war and everyone's role in it, the war ended before he got into uniform.

MULTIPLE CHOICE STUDY GUIDE/QUIZ QUESTIONS - *A Separate Peace*

Chapters 1-3

1. What two sites did the narrator go back to Devon to see?
   A. He went back to see the Butt Room and the dormitory.
   B. He went back to see the First Academy Building and the tree.
   C. He went back to see the Naguamsett River and the gym.
   D. He went back to see the Fields Beyond and the Crew House.

2. What is the relationship between the narrator, (Gene) and Phineas?
   A. They are best friends and roommates.
   B. They are rivals for first place in the class.
   C. They are brothers. Phineas is younger and constantly tries to live up to his brother's glowing reputation.
   D. They are soldiers who met during the war and share old school stories.

3. What unusual thing did Phineas talk Gene into doing?
   A. Phineas talked Gene into going on a bike trip from the school in New Hampshire to his home in Georgia.
   B. Phineas talked Gene into jumping from the limb of a tall tree into the river.
   C Phineas talked Gene into setting off smoke bombs one night in the dormitory of the nearby girls' school
   D. Phineas talked Gene into putting salt in all of the sugar bowls in the school cafeteria.

4. Why were the boys not punished for their actions?
   A. The Head Master knew it would ruin their chances of going to college.
   B. Gene's parents were on the board of trustees for the school and donated a lot of money. The headmaster didn't want to make a fuss.
   C. Finny had a gift of gab that made people overlook his faults and transgressions.
   D. The Head Master decided not to punish them since no one was hurt. He did lecture them about their responsibility as seniors.

5. Identify Mr. Prud-homme and Mr. Patch-Withers.
   A. Mr. Prud-homme was the crew coach, and Mr. Patch-Withers was the summer Head Master.
   B. Mr. Prud-homme was a substitute master for the summer, and Mr. Patch-Withers was the French teacher.
   C. Mr. Prud-homme was the summer Head Master, and Mr. Patch-Withers was the dormitory master.
   D. Mr. Prud-homme was a substitute master for the summer, and Mr. Patch-Withers was the stern, summer Head Master.

A Separate Peace Multiple Choice Study Questions Page 2

6. Why was the Super Suicide Society of the Summer Session created?
   A. It was created to talk the underclassmen out of taking an early service enlistment.
   B. It was created to get the boys to take flying lessons.
   C. It was created to help some of the boys who were depressed about the war, their grades, and other personal problems.
   D. It was created to formalize the jumping out of the tree ritual.

7. Gene said,"" I didn't need to feel any tremendous rush of gratitude towards Phineas." Why not?
   A. Phineas would never show any gratitude to Gene, so Gene did not want to show any either.
   B. Phineas had not done anything that Gene considered out of the ordinary.
   C. Gene figured he wouldn't have been there in the first place if Finny had not talked him into it.
   D. Gene and Phineas were such close friends that they did not need to express their feeling aloud to each other. They each knew what the other was thinking and feeling.

8. Why did Gene continue jumping out of the tree and going along with Phineas even though he didn't want to?
   A. Otherwise, he would have lost face with Phineas, and that was unthinkable.
   B. Phineas was blackmailing Gene with a secret from Gene's past and threatened to tell the others if Gene didn't jump.
   C. Gene was very insecure and did whatever he had to do to be popular.
   D. He didn't really like the school and was secretly hoping that he would get caught and expelled so he could enlist.

9. What was blitzball?
   A. It was an exercise routine the teachers were using to build the boys' physical stamina in anticipation of their enlisting after graduation.
   B. It was a game Phineas made up in which the odds were against the ball carrier and all of the players were enemies.
   C. It was a traditional Devon game that had been invented by members of Devon's first graduating class. Now playing it was required.
   D. It was a game the soldiers overseas had developed. A graduate who was in the Army visited the school and taught the boys to play.

10. In what way did Gene describe his memories of the war years?
    A. He associated events with the war battles that were going on.
    B. He talked about the songs that were popular.
    C. He described the courses he was taking.
    D. He gave the characteristics of America as he remembered them.

A Separate Peace Multiple Choice Study Questions Page 3

11. What did the swimming record incident show about Phineas?
    A. He was obsessed with getting recognition for his deeds.
    B. He had no respect for authority and school traditions.
    C. He only wanted to break the record for fun and for himself.
    D. He was really a talented swimmer who refused to join the team because he didn't want to practice.

12. "Exposing a sincere emotion like that at the Devon School was the next thing to suicide." What had Phineas just told Gene?
    A. Phineas had just told Gene that he had been abused as a child.
    B. Phineas had just told Gene that Gene was his best pal.
    C. Phineas had just told Gene that he didn't believe in God.
    D. Phineas had just told Gene that he did not support the war effort.

A Separate Peace Multiple Choice Study Questions Page 4

Chapters 4-5

13. What two realizations did Gene have about his relationship with Phineas?
    A. Phineas was jealous of Gene's being the head of the class and had deliberately set out to wreck his studies.
    B. Phineas didn't really like Gene but was using him to get help with studying and to borrow his (Gene's) clothes,
    C. They were friends only because they had been put in the same room; they had nothing in common that would carry the friendship over after they graduated from Devon.
    D. Gene didn't really like Phineas but was much too insecure to stand up to him.

14. Over what did Gene and Phineas argue?
    A. They argued over the height of the tree limb from the surface of the water.
    B. They argued over whether or not to admit an underclassman to their Suicide Society.
    C. They argued over lights out time in their room. Gene wanted to stay up late studying, and Phineas wanted to go to sleep early.
    D. They argued over whether Gene should study or go watch Leper Lepellier jump from the tree.

15. What happened to Phineas and why?
    A. Gene bounced on the limb he and Phineas were standing on. Phineas fell and badly broke his leg.
    B. Phineas got distracted by a joke Gene made. He lost his concentration, bellyflopped into the water, and knocked the breath out of himself.
    C. Phineas got a sudden fear of heights as he was preparing to jump. Gene climbed the tree and rescued him. The other boys lost their respect for Phineas, and the club was disbanded.
    D. The Head Master caught Phineas jumping from the tree. He put Phineas on restriction for the rest of the summer session.

16. Why didn't Gene tell Phineas the truth at the infirmary?
    A. Gene was afraid he would get expelled.
    B. Gene didn't remember exactly what had happened.
    C. Dr. Stanpole came in before Gene could tell him.
    D. Phineas was asleep, and Gene didn't want to wake him.

A Separate Peace Multiple Choice Study Questions Page 5

17. What was Phineas' reaction when Gene did confess?
    A. He laughed and said it was all a joke.
    B. At first he didn't want to believe it. Then he asked Gene to leave.
    C. He got hysterical, threw his crutches at Gene, and said he would never speak to Gene again.
    D. He said he had suspected it all along and that he would somehow get even with Gene.

A Separate Peace Multiple Choice Study Questions Page 6

Chapters 6-7

18. One character's reaction to Finny's accident was, "If you broke the rules, then they broke you." Who said this?
    A. Brinker
    B. Dr. Stanpole
    C. Phineas
    D. Gene

19. Identify Cliff Quackenbush.
    A. He was the rude, physically mature crew manager of the rowing team.
    B. He was Gene's new roommate, since Phineas was not coming back.
    C. He was Gene's rival in competing for the head of the class.
    D. He was a shy, awkward boy whom no one liked much.

20. How did Gene lose his job of Assistant Crew Manager?
    A. He got into a fight with the Crew Manager, and they ended up in the river.
    B. His grades went down and he was put on academic probation.
    C. He talked back to Mr. Ludsbury and lost his privileges for a semester.
    D. His father called the Head Master and said he wanted Gene to concentrate on his studies, that he could not participate in sports.

21. From whom was Gene's long distance call?
    A. It was from his father.
    B. It was from Phineas.
    C. It was from the dean of a college to which Gene had applied.
    D. It was from the draft recruiter.

22. How did Gene feel when Phineas said, "Listen, pal, if I can't play sports, you're going to play them for me?
    A. He felt forgiven and that he had found a way to make up for his meanness.
    B. He felt trapped, like he would be Finny's slave for the whole year.
    C. He felt resentful and thought that Phineas should admit to his handicap and get on with life.
    D. He felt excited because he always wanted the opportunity to excel at sports.

23. What idea did Brinker Hadley introduce?
    A. He said that Gene's parents paid extra to get him his own room.
    B. He said that they should all enlist together at the end of the year.
    C. He said that Gene bounced Finny out of the tree on purpose.
    D. He said that they should be allowed to smoke in their rooms.

A Separate Peace Multiple Choice Study Questions Page 7

24. Why did Gene leave the Butt Room without smoking a cigarette?
    A. He had a cold, and the smoke was bothering him.
    B. He was shaken by Brinker's insinuations about Finny's accident.
    C. He had promised his mother he would call her.
    D. He knew Mr. Ludsbury was on his way down to send the boys back to their rooms.

25. What good deed did the boys do?
    A. They tutored some of the young, poor boys in town.
    B. They cleared the railroad tracks of snow so the troop trains could go through.
    C. They donated their entertainment money to the Red Cross.
    D. They took food and water to people who could not go out due to the weather.

26. What did Gene say about Brinker as he tried to spare Leper's feelings when the gang met him after their good deed was done?
    A. He said that Brinker would believe anything he was told.
    B. He said that Brinker would probably brag for a month about helping out the war effort.
    C. He said that Brinker was good at heart; he just had a rude streak.
    D. He said that Brinker couldn't be put off with half a story.

27. Who decided to enlist?
    A. Brinker and Gene decided to enlist.
    B. Mr. Ludsbury decided to enlist.
    C. Forrester and Quackenbush decided to enlist.
    D. Lepellier and Chet decided to enlist.

28. Why did Gene not enlist?
    A. He was against the war and refused to fight.
    B. His vision was too poor and he could not get in.
    C. Phineas returned.
    D. He didn't know what he wanted to do, so he was going to wait and get drafted after graduation.

A Separate Peace Multiple Choice Study Questions Page 8

Chapters 8-9

29. Of what did Finny try to convince Gene about the war?
    A. The Germans were going to invade the United States soon.
    B. There was no war; it was made up by fat old men.
    C. His (Finny's) leg would have healed enough by graduation that he could also enlist.
    D. Hitler would probably win.

30. For what event did Finny want to train Gene? What was wrong with that plan?
    A. Finny wanted to train Gene for the 1944 Olympics, but they had been canceled because of the war.
    B. Finny wanted to train Gene for the Boston Marathon, but the Head Master would not let them leave campus.
    C. Finny wanted to train Gene to be class valedictorian, but Gene's grades were not high enough.
    D. Finny wanted to train Gene to take the lead in the senior class play, but Gene could not remember his lines.

31. Why did Phineas decide that Mr. Ludsbury didn't know the truth (according to Phineas) about the war?
    A. Mr. Ludsbury was mentally ill.
    B. Mr. Ludsbury was a traitor.
    C. Mr. Ludsbury was not bright enough.
    D. Mr. Ludsbury was thin.

32. Who was the first of Gene's gang to actually enlist?
    A. Brinker was the first to enlist.
    B. Quackenbush was the first to enlist.
    C. Leper was the first to enlist.
    D. Gene was the first to enlist.

33. What effect did the enlistment have on the boys at Devon?
    A. They became fearful for the enlistee's safety.
    B. It established their link with the war.
    C. They all wanted to follow the enlistee's example.
    D. They became very quiet and studious.

34. What event did Phineas invent?
    A. He invented the Winter Carnival.
    B. He invented the Tournament of the Minds.
    C. He invented the Devon Olympics to Benefit the Soldiers.
    D. He invented the Midnight Ice Follies.

A Separate Peace Multiple Choice Study Questions Page 9

35. From whom was Gene's telegram, and what was the message?"
    A. It was from Finny's parents. They asked him to keep an eye on Phineas and not let him do anything dangerous.
    B. It was from the recruiter. It said that Gene would have to decide which branch to enlist in within the next two weeks.
    C. It was from Leper. It said he had escaped and needed help.
    D. It was from the college he wanted to attend. It said he had won a full scholarship.

A Separate Peace Multiple Choice Study Questions Page 10

Chapters 10-11
36. What happened to Leper?
    A. He was injured during training and could not walk.
    B. He was about to be sent overseas, and he came home to say goodbye.
    C. The army found out he was under age, and they said he couldn't stay.
    D. He went AWOL because he was about to get a discharge for mentally ill soldiers.

37. How did Gene react to Leper's description of what happened to him?
    A. Gene felt sorry for Leper. He offered to help any way he could.
    B. Gene didn't believe it. He thought Leper was playing a practical joke on all of them.
    C. Gene thought it was the ski troop's fault. He decided to help Leper file a formal complain against them. He also decided he would never enlist himself.
    D. Gene didn't want to hear it. He told Leper to shut up and then he ran away and left Leper alone.

38. Why did Gene want only to see Phineas?
    A. He knew Phineas would have good suggestions about helping Leper.
    B. Phineas was removed enough from the war to be a safe harbor for Gene.
    C. Phineas would be able to find the humor in the situation and cheer Gene up.
    D. Phineas' father was a lawyer and would know how to help.

39. Brinker said, "What's the matter with our class anyway? It isn't even June yet and we've already got two men sidelined for the duration." Who and what was he talking about?
    A. He was talking about Gene and Phineas and the upcoming Olympics.
    B. He was talking about Leper and Phil Latham, who had quit school early.
    C. He was talking about Phineas and Leper and their inability to fight in the war.
    D. He was talking about Quackenbush and Gene not working together on the crew team.

40. How did Leper's illness affect Phineas?
    A. It made him afraid he would have similar problems if he didn't face up to his handicap.
    B. It made the war real and inescapable. He realized he would not be part of any physical contest.
    C. He had no tolerance for any kind of weakness. It made him ridicule Leper as a coward and sissy.
    D. It brought out a sense of compassion that he had never realized he had.

A Separate Peace Multiple Choice Study Questions Page 11

41. Which describes Brinker's and Gene's views of Finny's disability?
    A. They both thought the boys should tease Finny to help him face his disability and get on with his life.
    B. Gene thought they should help Finny face his disability, but Brinker thought they should ignore it and hope it would get better.
    C. They both thought everyone should pity Finny and offer to help him as much as possible.
    D. Brinker thought they should to help him face his disability and get on with his life. Gene thought they should ignore it and hope it would get better.

42. Where did Brinker take Gene and Finny? Why?
    A. He took them to the tree to talk about the accident.
    B. He took them to the First Building. He had a group of students who were to investigate Gene's role in Finny's accident.
    C. He took them to the head master's office to meet a Navy recruiter who had a position for Finny doing office work. Brinker thought it would cheer Finny up to be able to be of some use during the war.
    D. He took them to Dr. Stanpole's office. Dr. Stanpole had contacted a bone specialist in Boston and wanted Gene to take Finny there for some experimental therapy.

43. Why did Finny rush out of the room?
    A. He heard footsteps and didn't want to be caught in the building after hours.
    B. He wanted to go down to the river because he always did his best thinking there.
    C. He didn't want to face the fact that Gene was responsible for the accident.
    D. He was furious. He knew he would beat Gene with his cane if he stayed in the room.

44. What happened to Finny after he ran out of the room?
    A. He went into a rage and broke all of the windows in the hallway.
    B. He sat under a tree in the courtyard and cried.
    C. He began laughing hysterically. The boys finally calmed him down and helped him return to his room.
    D. He fell down the marble stairs and broke his leg again.

A Separate Peace Multiple Choice Study Questions Page 12

Chapters 12-13

45. Why didn't Gene do anything to help with Phineas after the episode?
    A. The doctor had forbidden him to see Phineas.
    B. He felt responsible and thought that Phineas would get more upset at seeing him.
    C. He was too worried about his own status with the other boys. He went into seclusion in his room until things settled down.
    D. The other boys ignored him. Brinker told him they didn't need his help.

46. What did Gene do?
    A. He sneaked into the infirmary to apologize to Phineas.
    B. He went to the school's minister to talk.
    C. He called Finny's parents and talked to them.
    D. He went to the tree and jumped out of it again.

47. What was Gene's opinion of Finny's place in the war?
    A. He would be a good soldier even if he were somewhat handicapped.
    B. He would be better off supporting the effort behind the scenes, perhaps by visiting with disabled soldiers in the hospital.
    C. He would not be any good in the war even if he had full use of his leg because he was too sociable.
    D. He would be an inspiration to other soldiers if he pursued in the face of his disability.

48. What finally happened to Phineas?
    A. He was released from the hospital and resumed his studies.
    B. He died because bone marrow got into his blood stream and stopped his heart.
    C. His leg had to be amputated. He became so depressed that his parents sent him to a rest home in Boston for a few months.
    D. He recovered partial use of his leg but ended his friendship with Gene.

ANSWER KEY - MULTIPLE CHOICE STUDY/QUIZ QUESTIONS
A Separate Peace

Chapters 1-3	Chapters 4-5	Chapters 6-7	Chapters 8-9
1. B	13. A	18. D	29. B
2. A	14. D	19. A	30. A
3. B	15. A	20. A	31. D
4. C	16. C	21. B	32. C
5. D	17. B	22. A	33. B
6. D		23. C	34. A
7. C		24. B	35. C
8. A		25. B	
9. B		26. D	
10. D		27. A	
11. C		28. C	
12. B			

Chapters 10 - 13
36. D
37. D
38. B
39. C
40. B
41. D
42. B
43. C
44. D
45. B
46. A
47. C
48. B
49. A

PREREADING VOCABULARY WORKSHEETS

VOCABULARY - *A Separate Peace*

<u>Chapters 1-3</u>
Part I: Using Prior Knowledge and Contextual Clues

Below are the sentences in which the vocabulary words appear in the text. Read the sentence. Use any clues you can find in the sentence combined with your prior knowledge, and write what you think the underlined words mean on the lines provided.

1. In the deep, <u>tacit</u> way in which feeling becomes stronger than thought

_____

2. . . . <u>capacious</u> Greek Revival temples lined the street, as impressive and just as forbidding as ever.

_____

3. It is the beauty of small areas of order--a large yard, a group of trees, three similar dormitories, a circle of old houses--living together in <u>contentious</u> harmony.

_____

4. Standing on this limb, you could by a <u>prodigious</u> effort jump far enough out into the river for safety.

_____

5. . . . trying hard not to sound as <u>inane</u> in our conversation with the four present Masters and their wives as they sounded to us.

_____

6. I never got <u>inured</u> to the jumping. At every meeting the limb seemed higher, thinner, the deeper water harder to reach.

_____

7. There was something <u>inebriating</u> in the suppleness of this feat. When I thought about it my head felt a little dizzy and my stomach began to tingle.

_____

A Separate Peace Vocabulary: Chapters 1-3 Continued

Part II: Determining the Meaning Match the vocabulary words to their dictionary definitions. If there are words for which you cannot figure out the definition by contextual clues and by process of elimination, look them up in a dictionary.

___ 1. tacit   A. Spacious; roomy
___ 2. capacious   B. Lacking in sense or substance
___ 3. contentious   C. Intoxicating
___ 4. prodigious   D. Not spoken
___ 5. inane   E. To get used to something undesirable
___ 6. inured   F. Quarrelsome; not getting along
___ 7. inebriating   G. Extraordinary; impressively great

A Separate Peace Vocabulary   Chapters 4-5

Part I: Using Prior Knowledge and Contextual Clues
   Below are the sentences in which the vocabulary words appear in the text. Read the sentence. Use any clues you can find in the sentence combined with your prior knowledge, and write what you think the underlined words mean on the lines provided.

1. . . . dead gray waves hissing mordantly along the beach, which was gray and dead-looking itself.

   _____

2. The beach shed its deadness and became a spectral gray-white . . . and finally it was totally white and stainless, as pure as the shores of Eden.

   _____

3. You are both even in enmity. You are both coldly driving ahead for yourselves alone.

   _____

4. There was a latent freshness in the air, as though spring were returning in the middle of the summer.

   _____

5. "If he jumps out of that tree I'm Mahatma Ghandi." . . . He had a way of turning cliches inside out like that.

   _____

6. "Yes." I let this drop curtly to bar him from telling me what to do about my work.

   _____

7. I went south for a month's vacation in my home town and spent it in an atmosphere of reverie and unreality, as though I had lived that month once already and had not been interested by it the first time either.

   _____

A Separate Peace Vocabulary: Chapters 4-5 Continued

Part II: Determining the Meaning   Match the vocabulary words to their dictionary definitions. If there are words for which you cannot figure out the definition by contextual clues and by process of elimination, look them up in a dictionary.

___ 8. mordantly
___ 9. spectral
___ 10. enmity
___ 11. latent
___ 12. cliches
___ 13. curtly
___ 14. reverie

A. Present but not developed or active
B. Rudely brief or abruptly
C. Ghostly
D. Daydreaming
E. Bitingly sarcastic or painful
F. Trite or overused expressions
G. Deep-rooted often mutual hatred

A Separate Peace Vocabulary: Chapters 6-7

Part I: Using Prior Knowledge and Contextual Clues

Below are the sentences in which the vocabulary words appear in the text. Read the sentence. Use any clues you can find in the sentence combined with your prior knowledge, and write what you think the underlined words mean on the lines provided.

1. We had been an <u>idiosyncratic</u>, leaderless band in the summer, undirected except by the eccentric notions of Phineas.

_____

2. Then, an <u>infinitesimal</u> veering of the canoe, and the line of his body would break . . . and Phineas would tumble into the water . . . .

_____

3. There is no such position officially, but it sometimes came into existence through necessity, and was the opposite of a <u>sinecure</u>. It was all work and no advantages.

_____

4. He had a tough <u>bantam</u> body, easily detectable under the tight sweat shirt he wore.

_____

5. He bent down to tighten the lacings on a <u>puttee</u>.

_____

6. I bounced <u>zestfully</u> up the dormitory stairs.

_____

Part II: Determining the Meaning   Match the vocabulary words to their dictionary definitions.

___ 15. idiosyncratic   A. Lower leg covering
___ 16. infinitesimal   B. Peculiar
___ 17. sinecure   C. Small but aggressive & spirited
___ 18. bantam   D. With spirit and energy
___ 19. puttee   E. Immeasurably small
___ 20. zestfully   F. A paid position requiring little work

A Separate Peace Vocabulary: Chapters 8-9

Part I: Using Prior Knowledge and Contextual Clues

Below are the sentences in which the vocabulary words appear in the text. Read the sentence. Use any clues you can find in the sentence combined with your prior knowledge, and write what you think the underlined words mean on the lines provided.

1. . . . he was always speaking when his thoughts were somewhere else, asking <u>rhetorical</u> questions and echoing other people's words.

_____

2. "He wants to know if I'll . . . enlist." It was the ultimate question for all seventeen-year-olds that year, and it drove Brinker's <u>insinuations</u> from every mind but mine.

_____

3. The school had been largely rebuilt with a massive bequest from an oil family . . . in a peculiar style of Puritan grandeur, as though Versailles had been modified for the needs of a Sunday school. This <u>opulent</u> sobriety betrayed the divided nature of the school . . . .

_____

4. I was sure that this was his goal, to <u>mull</u> over those lost glories.

_____

5. I had prepared myself for that, and even thought of several positive, uplifting <u>aphorisms</u> to cheer him up.

_____

6. But since we were so far out of the line of fire, the chief <u>sustenance</u> for any sense of the war was mental.

_____

7. I mumbled some <u>abashed</u> answer, but it was Phineas who made the clear response.

_____

A Separate Peace Vocabulary: Chapters 8-9 Continued

8. Finny had regretfully given up the plan of inviting the school band to supply music. . . . Chet in any case was an improvement over that <u>cacophony</u>.

_____

Part II: Determining the Meaning   Match the vocabulary words to their dictionary definitions. If there are words for which you cannot figure out the definition by contextual clues and by process of elimination, look them up in a dictionary.

___ 21. rhetorical   A. Concerned primarily with show or effect
___ 22. insinuations   B. Discordant sounds
___ 23. opulent   C. Support for life
___ 24. mull   D. Implications
___ 25. aphorisms   E. Ashamed or uneasy; disconcerted
___ 26. sustenance   F. Luxurious
___ 27. abashed   G. Short statements of truth; adages
___ 28. cacophony   H. To go over extensively in the mind; ponder

A Separate Peace Vocabulary Chapters 10-11

Part I: Using Prior Knowledge and Contextual Clues
   Below are the sentences in which the vocabulary words appear in the text. Read the sentence. Use any clues you can find in the sentence combined with your prior knowledge, and write what you think the underlined words mean on the lines provided.

1. Programs scheduled to culminate in two years became outmoded in six months . . . .

_____

2. I and those of my year were preeminently eligible for that.

_____

3. I imperceptibly nodded and shook my head, yes-and-no.

_____

4. These were . . . on the edge of the woods which, however English in name, were in my mind primevally American, reaching in unbroken forests far to the north, into the great northern wilderness.

_____

5. Who else could have inveigled twenty people to the farthest extremity of the school to throw snowballs at each other?

_____

6. Lost two thousand years in the past, master of a dead language and a dead empire, the bane and bore of schoolboys, Caesar he believed to be more of a tyrant at Devon than he had ever been in Rome.

_____

A Separate Peace Vocabulary: Chapters 10-11 Continued

Part II: Determining the Meaning

You have tried to figure out the meanings of the vocabulary words for Chapters 10 - 11. Now match the vocabulary words to their dictionary definitions. If there are words for which you cannot figure out the definition by contextual clues and by process of elimination, look them up in a dictionary.

___ 29. culminate   A. Belonging to the earliest ages; ancient
___ 30. preeminently   B. Coaxed
___ 31. imperceptibly   C. Impossible to detect with ordinary senses
___ 32. inveigled   D. A deadly poison; cause of ruin
___ 33. bane   E. Come to an end
___ 34. primevally   F. Outstandingly

A Separate Peace Vocabulary Chapters 12-13

Part I: Using Prior Knowledge and Contextual Clues
   Below are the sentences in which the vocabulary words appear in the text. Read the sentence. Use any clues you can find in the sentence combined with your prior knowledge, and write what you think the underlined words mean on the lines provided.

1. Perhaps it was just the incongruity of seeing him aloft and stricken, since he was by nature someone who carried others.

   _____

2. There was something innately strange about it, as though there had always been an inner core to the gym which I had never perceived before, quite different from its generally accepted appearance.

   _____

3. My brief burst of animosity, lasting only a second, a part of a second, something which came before I could recognize it and was gone before I knew it had possessed me, what was that in the midst of this holocaust?

   _____

4. I no longer had any qualms about that, although I couldn't help being glad that it would not be at Devon, at anywhere like Devon, that I would have that.

   _____

Part II: Determining the Meaning
   You have tried to figure out the meanings of the vocabulary words for Chapters 12 - 13. Now match the vocabulary words to their dictionary definitions. If there are words for which you cannot figure out the definition by contextual clues and by process of elimination, look them up in a dictionary.

   ___ 35. incongruity   A. Inborn; inherently
   ___ 36. innately   B. Doubts
   ___ 37. animosity   C. Not corresponding in character or kind
   ___ 38. qualms   D. Bitter hostility

ANSWER KEY - VOCABULARY
A Separate Peace

Chapters 1 - 3	Chapters 4 - 5	Chapters 6 - 7
1. D	8. E	15. B
2. A	9. C	16. E
3. F	10. G	17. F
4. G	11. A	18. C
5. B	12. F	19. A
6. E	13. B	20. D
7. C	14. D	

Chapters 8 - 9	Chapters 10 - 11	Chapters 12 - 13
21. A	29. E	35. C
22. D	30. F	36. A
23. F	31. C	37. D
24. H	32. B	38. B
25. G	33. D	
26. C	34. A	
27. E		
28. B		

DAILY LESSONS

LESSON ONE

Objectives
1. To introduce the *A Separate Peace* unit
2. To distribute books and other related materials
3. To preview the study questions for chapters 1-3
4. To familiarize students with the vocabulary for chapters 1-3

NOTE: Prior to this lesson, you need to get enough newspapers for everyone in your class. Often local newspaper offices will give out newspapers free for educational purposes. Check with them. If they will not give you the current day's newspaper, perhaps they would give you leftover papers from the day before.

Activity #1

Distribute one newspaper to each student in your class. Most papers have hard news, editorials, sports, features/entertainment, obituaries, and, of course, advertising. Write these categories up on the board and explain to students what each is. Using the newspapers you have distributed, show students an example of each category. Collect the newspapers for use later in the unit.

Activity #2

Distribute the Class Project Assignment Sheet. Discuss the directions in detail.

Activity #3

Distribute the materials students will use in this unit. Explain in detail how students are to use these materials.

Study Guides Students should read the study guide questions for each reading assignment prior to beginning the reading assignment to get a feeling for what events and ideas are important in the section they are about to read. After reading the section, students will (as a class or individually) answer the questions to review the important events and ideas from that section of the book. Students should keep the study guides as study materials for the unit test.

Vocabulary Prior to reading a reading assignment, students will do vocabulary work related to the section of the book they are about to read. Following the completion of the reading of the book, there will be a vocabulary review of all the words used in the vocabulary assignments. Students should keep their vocabulary work as study materials for the unit test.

Reading Assignment Sheet   You need to fill in the reading assignment sheet to let students know by when their reading has to be completed. You can either write the assignment sheet up on a side blackboard or bulletin board and leave it there for students to see each day or you can "ditto" copies for each student to have. In either case, you should advise students to become very familiar with the reading assignments so they know what is expected of them.

Extra Activities Center   The resource sections of this unit contain suggestions for an extra library of related books and articles in your classroom as well as crossword and word search puzzles. Make an extra activities center in your room where you will keep these materials for students to use. (Bring the books and articles in from the library and keep several copies of the puzzles on hand). Explain to students that these materials are available for students to use when they finish reading assignments or other class work early.

Nonfiction Assignment Sheet   Explain to students that they each are to read at least one newspaper article from your local newspaper each week during the unit, a total of four articles. Students will fill out a nonfiction assignment sheet after completing the reading to help you evaluate their reading experiences and to help the students think about and evaluate their own reading experiences. To make sure students do one per week instead of doing four at the last minute, collect one Nonfiction Reading Assignment Sheet each week from each student.

Books   Each school has its own rules and regulations regarding student use of school books. Advise students of the procedures that are normal for your school.

Activity #3
Preview the study questions and have students do the vocabulary work for Chapters 1-3 of *A Separate Peace*. If students do not finish this assignment during this class period, they should complete it prior to the next class meeting.

CLASS PROJECT ASSIGNMENT SHEET - *A Separate Peace*

PROMPT

The book you are about to read, *A Separate Peace*, is about what happened to two friends at school one summer in the early years of World War II. Living at the school, they were, for the most part, sheltered from direct contact with the war. Theirs was a world of studies and games, sports and fun--even though the rest of the world was at war; thus, one level of meaning for the title of the book.

During World War II, prior to The Age of Television, people had three main sources of news: radios, newspapers, and word of mouth. Judging from the first activity we did today, you have probably guessed that the source we will be concerned with for this project is the newspaper. We're concentrating on the newspaper for two reasons:

1. It fits in well with the time-frame of the novel. Newspapers were very important during World War II. The boys at Devon School would have preferred to maintain their separate peace, but news kept encroaching on their oasis.

2. The boys were at school, and most schools publish some sort of a newspaper to inform students about what is going on at the school, to act as a historical record of the times, and to give journalism students practical experience at journalistic writing.

THE ASSIGNMENT

You are writers and editors. At various times throughout this unit, you will be asked to write hard news stories, editorials, feature and sports stories, advertisements, and even obituaries. Everyone in the class will write and submit copy for each assignment, and then the class will evaluate the assignments and determine which ones will be published in our newspaper, *The Devon Times*. The Editor-in-Chief (teacher) will have final say as to what will be published. Each student must have at least one contribution published. All of your assignments will relate to the novel *A Separate Peace*--the characters and the events.

NONFICTION ASSIGNMENT SHEET
(To be completed after reading the required nonfiction article)

Name _____ Date _____

Title of Nonfiction Read _____

Written By _____ Publication Date _____

I. Factual Summary: Write a short summary of the piece you read.

II. Vocabulary
    1. With which vocabulary words in the piece did you encounter some degree of difficulty?

    2. How did you resolve your lack of understanding with these words?

III. Interpretation: What was the main point the author wanted you to get from reading his work?

IV. Criticism
    1. With which points of the piece did you agree or find easy to accept? Why?

    2. With which points of the piece did you disagree or find difficult to believe? Why?

V. Personal Response: What do you think about this piece? OR How does this piece influence your ideas?

LESSON TWO

Objectives
1. To read chapters 1-3
2. To do the prereading work for chapters 4-5
3. To evaluate students' oral reading

Activity

Have students read chapters 1-3 of *A Separate Peace* out loud in class. You probably know the best way to get readers with your class; pick students at random, ask for volunteers, or use whatever method works best for your group. If you have not yet completed an oral reading evaluation for your students this marking period, this would be a good opportunity to do so. A form is included with this unit for your convenience.

Assignment

If students do not complete reading chapters 1-3 in class, they should do so prior to your next class meeting. Also prior to your next class period, students should preview the study questions and do the prereading vocabulary work for chapters 4-5.

ORAL READING EVALUATION - *A Separate Peace*

Name _____ Class____ Date _____

SKILL	EXCELLENT	GOOD	AVERAGE	FAIR	POOR
Fluency	5	4	3	2	1
Clarity	5	4	3	2	1
Audibility	5	4	3	2	1
Pronunciation	5	4	3	2	1
_____	5	4	3	2	1
_____	5	4	3	2	1

Total _____   Grade _____

Comments:

LESSON THREE

Objectives
1. To review the main events and ideas from chapters 1-3
2. To read chapters 4-5
3. To do the prereading work for chapters 6-7

Activity #1
Give students a few minutes to formulate answers for the study guide questions for chapters 1-3 and then discuss the answers to the questions in detail. Write the answers on the board or overhead transparency so students can have the correct answers for study purposes. NOTE: It is a good practice in public speaking and leadership skills for individual students to take charge of leading the discussions of the study questions. Perhaps a different student could go to the front of the class and lead the discussion each day that the study questions are discussed during this unit. Of course, the teacher should guide the discussion when appropriate and be sure to fill in any gaps the students leave.

Activity #2
Have students read chapters 4-5 of *A Separate Peace* orally in class. You probably know the best way to get readers with your class; pick students at random, ask for volunteers, or use whatever method works best for your group.

Assignment: If students do not finish reading chapters 4-5 by the end of the class, they should do so prior to the next class period. They should also preview the study questions for chapters 6-7 of *A Separate Peace* and to do the related vocabulary work.

LESSON FOUR

Objectives
1. To review the main ideas and events from chapters 4-5
2. To read chapters 6-7

Activity #1
Give students a few minutes to formulate answers for the study guide questions for chapters 4-5 and then discuss the answers to the questions in detail. Write the answers on the board or overhead transparency so students can have the correct answers for study purposes.

Activity #2
Have students read chapters 6-7 of *A Separate Peace* orally in class. You probably know the best way to get readers with your class; pick students at random, ask for volunteers, or use whatever method works best for your group. If students do not finish reading chapters 6-7 by the end of the class, they should do so prior to Lesson Six. (Give students a day and a date.)

LESSON FIVE

<u>Objectives</u>
1. To give students the opportunity to practice writing to inform
2. To have students practice writing a hard news story
3. To give the teacher the opportunity to evaluate students' writing skills
4. To review the main events of the story so far

<u>Activity #1</u>

Distribute the newspapers you used in Lesson One. Ask students what a hard news story is. See how many students remember that from Lesson One. Ask students to give the headline for one of the hard news stories in your newspapers. Look at that story in detail. Show students how the caption and first line(s) hook the reader, how the story is completely factual and non-partial. (Let's hope it is; these days so many stories are slanted . . . !). Show students how the article covers the traditional "who, what, when, where, why" information.

Look at a second example if you think your students need reinforcement.

Summarize the traits of a hard news story by listing them on the board:
1. Hooks the reader with the caption and/or first line(s)
2. Is completely factual; no opinions are given
3. Answers "who, what, when, where, why and how"

<u>Activity #2</u>

Distribute Writing Assignment #1 and discuss the directions in detail. Allow the remaining class time for students to complete the assignment. Tell students when their work will be collected.

<u>Follow-Up:</u> After you have graded the assignments, have a writing conference with the students. (This unit schedules one in Lesson Eight.) After the writing conference, allow students to revise their papers using your suggestions and corrections. Give them about three days from the date they receive their papers to complete the revision. I suggest grading the revisions on an A-C-E scale (all revisions well-done, some revisions made, few or no revisions made). This will speed your grading time and still give some credit for the students' efforts.

WRITING ASSIGNMENT #1 - *A Separate Peace*

PROMPT
So far in the book, there have been several newsworthy events. Your assignment is to take one of those events and write a hard news story about it.

PREWRITING
Browse back through your study guides or the book and make a list of all the events you believe were newsworthy. After carefully considering the list, choose the one event you would most like to report.

On your scribble paper, write down " who, what, when, where, why, and how" down the left side of the page. Write the appropriate information about your event next to each.

Next, decide on a caption for your article. Jot down several ideas and then decide which is best.

DRAFTING
Write your caption at the top of your page. Keep one of the hard news newspaper articles handy as you begin to write your article. Pattern yours after that one. The first paragraph should give all the basic information from the list you made on your scratch paper. The following paragraphs should fill in the details. REMEMBER TO BE OBJECTIVE: NO OPINIONS-- ONLY FACTS.

PROMPT
When you finish the rough draft of your paper, ask a student who sits near you to read it. After reading your rough draft, he/she should tell you what he/she liked best about your work, which parts were difficult to understand, and ways in which your work could be improved. Reread your paper considering your critic's comments and make the corrections you think are necessary.

PROOFREADING
Do a final proofreading of your paper double-checking your grammar, spelling, organization, and the clarity of your ideas.

LESSON SIX

Objectives
1. To review the main ideas of chapters 6-7
2. To preview the study questions for chapters 8-9
3. To read chapters 8-9

Activity #1
Quiz - Distribute quizzes for chapters 6-7 and give students about 10 minutes to complete them. (NOTE: The quizzes may either be the short answer study guides or the multiple choice version.) Have students exchange papers. Grade the quizzes as a class. Collect the papers for recording the grades. (If you used the multiple choice version as a quiz, take a few minutes to discuss the answers for the short answer version if your students are using the short answer version for their study guides.)

Activity #2
Tell students that prior to the next class period they should have completed the prereading and reading work for chapters 8-9. They should take time now to preview the study questions and do the vocabulary work, and then read silently for the remainder of the class time.

LESSON SEVEN

Objectives
1. To review the main events of chapters 8-9
2. To assign the pre-reading, vocabulary and reading work for chapters 10-13

Activity #1
Give students a few minutes to formulate answers for the study guide questions for chapters 8-9 and then discuss the answers to the questions in detail. Write the answers on the board or overhead transparency so students can have the correct answers for study purposes.

Activity #2
Tell students that prior to the next class meeting they must have completed the pre-reading, vocabulary and reading work for chapters 10-13. Students may have the remainder of this period to work on this assignment.

NOTE: If you, the teacher, have not completed grading/evaluating Writing Assignment #1, use this time to work on that so you will be ready for the writing conferences in the next class period.

LESSON EIGHT

Objectives
1. To evaluate students' writing
2. To have students revise their writing assignment 1 papers
3. To review the main ideas and events of chapters 10-13.

Activity #1
Give students a few minutes to formulate answers for the study guide questions for chapters 10-13, and then discuss the answers to the questions in detail. Write the answers on the board or overhead transparency so students can have the correct answers for study purposes.

Activity #2
Call students to your desk (or some other private area) to discuss their papers from Writing Assignment #1. A Writing Evaluation Form is included with this unit to help structure your conferences.

While waiting to be called for a conference, students may work on the assignment made in Lesson Seven. After students have had a writing conference with you, they should return to their seats and begin working on their writing assignment revisions while your suggestions are fresh in their minds. Students should submit their revisions to you at the end of this class period.

Having all students make the revisions and resubmit good copies does three things. It gives the student a sense that he/she can write something worthwhile. It gives the student practice fixing his/her errors so he/she knows what to avoid next time. It gives the student a good composition that has a chance to be accepted for publication in your newspaper.

WRITING EVALUATION FORM - *A Separate Peace*

Name _____ Date _____

Writing Assignment #1 for the *A Separate Peace* unit   Grade _____

Circle One For Each Item:

Letter Format: corrections noted on paper

Character Analysis: excellent   good   fair   poor

Grammar: corrections noted on paper

Spelling: corrections noted on paper

Punctuation: corrections noted on paper

Legibility: excellent   good   fair   poor

Strengths:

Weaknesses:

Comments/Suggestions:

LESSON NINE

Objectives
1. To determine which of the hard news stories are worthy of publication
2. To give students the opportunity to express their personal opinions
3. To give the teacher the opportunity to evaluate students' writing skills
4. To have students practice writing an editorial

Activity #1

Divide your class into groups of four or five students. Give each group four or five of the hard news stories to evaluate. Be sure to take student names off of the papers so the judging will be impartial. Try not to give any group the papers for any of its group members.

Each student should read one composition orally to the remainder of the group. After all the compositions have been read, students should rank the compositions best (1), second-best (2), third-best (3), fourth-best (4) and fifth place (5). Judgement should be based on how well the composition fulfilled the requirements set up in Writing Assignment #1. (Was the caption an attention-grabber? Were all the who, what . . . questions answered? Did the author stick strictly to facts without any opinions?) The rank should be written on the papers.

Activity #2

Collect all of the papers ranked 1. In the event that you have more than one story on the same topic, read the choices to the class and have the class vote as to which story is better for publication. If all the compositions cover the same story, vote on which one should be used. Then, collect all of the papers ranked 2. Go through the same process. Ask then if anyone has compositions about topics other than those covered so far. If so, collect those and repeat the process. In the end, you should have one paper for publication about each major incident in the novel through chapter 7.

Activity #3

Distribute Writing Assignment #2. Discuss the directions in detail and give students the remainder of the class time to work on it.

NOTE: These assignments will go through the same process as Writing Assignment #1. There will be writing conferences, students should make the revisions, the revisions will be ranked, and the class will vote on which ones should be published.

NOTE: Distribute the daily newspapers you have been using. When you read through the PROMPT section of the assignment sheet, stop and read some of the editorials in the newspaper with your class. Point out the major differences between hard news stories and editorials.

WRITING ASSIGNMENT #2 - *A Separate Peace*

PROMPT
Unlike hard news stories, editorials are characterized by being opinions. They are the author's comments about some aspect of our world. Take a few minutes to review some editorials from your local newspaper so you will get the feel for what an editorial is and how one is written.

Your assignment is to write an editorial about something relating to *A Separate Peace*.

PREWRITING AND DRAFTING
First, find a topic. Here are some suggestions:
1. Give your opinions about any one character from the book
2. Give your opinions about the book as a whole
3. Give your opinions about an event in the book
4. Give your opinions about the treatment of a topic in the book (the war, education, friendship, growing up, human nature, etc.

You don't have to choose one of these; if there is some other aspect of the book you would like to voice an opinion about, please do so.

After you find a topic, you need to make some notes about what you want to say, and organize your notes in a logical manner. Directions for prewriting and writing can't be very specific because you all will be writing on a variety of topics which would involve a variety of different directions. Reread some editorials for ideas as to how to approach different topics. Raise your hand for help.

PROMPT
When you finish the rough draft of your paper, ask a student who sits near you to read it. After reading your rough draft, he/she should tell you what he/she liked best about your work, which parts were difficult to understand, and ways in which your work could be improved. Reread your paper considering your critic's comments and make the corrections you think are necessary.

PROOFREADING
Do a final proofreading of your paper double-checking your grammar, spelling, organization, and the clarity of your ideas.

LESSON TEN

Objective
    To review all of the vocabulary work done in this unit

Activity
    Choose one (or more) of the vocabulary review activities listed below and spend your class period as directed in the activity. Some of the materials for these review activities are located in the Vocabulary Resource section in this unit.

VOCABULARY REVIEW ACTIVITIES

1. Divide your class into two teams and have an old-fashioned spelling or definition bee.

2. Give each of your students (or students in groups of two, three or four) *A Separate Peace* Vocabulary Word Search Puzzle. The person (group) to find all of the vocabulary words in the puzzle first wins.

3. Give students *A Separate Peace* Vocabulary Word Search Puzzle without the word list. The person or group to find the most vocabulary words in the puzzle wins.

4. Use *A Separate Peace* Vocabulary Crossword Puzzle. Put the puzzle onto a transparency on the overhead projector (so everyone can see it), and do the puzzle together as a class.

5. Give students *A Separate Peace* Vocabulary Matching Worksheet to do.

6. Divide your class into two teams. Use the *A Separate Peace* vocabulary words with their letters jumbled as a word list. Student 1 from Team A faces off against Student 1 from Team B. You write the first jumbled word on the board. The first student (1A or 1B) to unscramble the word wins the chance for his/her team to score points. If 1A wins the jumble, go to student 2A and give him/her a definition. He/she must give you the correct spelling of the vocabulary word which fits that definition. If he/she does, Team A scores a point, and you give student 3A a definition for which you expect a correctly spelled matching vocabulary word. Continue giving Team A definitions until some team member makes an incorrect response. An incorrect response sends the game back to the jumbled-word face off, this time with students 2A and 2B. Instead of repeating giving definitions to the first few students of each team, continue with the student after the one who gave the last incorrect response on the team. For example, if Team B wins the jumbled-word face-off, and student 5B gave the last incorrect answer for Team B, you would start this round of definition questions with student 6B, and so on. The team with the most points wins!

7. Have students write a story in which they correctly use as many vocabulary words as possible. Have students read their compositions orally. Post the most original compositions on your bulletin board.

LESSON ELEVEN

Objectives
1. To give students a chance to work together in small groups to exchange ideas and find information
2. To point out some of the major themes of the novel
3. To get students to think about the novel and come up with their own ideas about each theme in order to encourage critical and logical thinking
4. To evaluate students' writing skills and give them suggestions about how to improve their editorials

Activity #1

Divide your class into groups - one group for each of the following ideas:
1. War
2. Foreshadowing & irony
3. Character analysis of Gene
4. Character analysis of Finny
5. Character analysis of others (Leper, Brinker, Ludsbury, Quackenbush)
6. Role of sports/contests/activities
7. Religion/God/prayer
8. Symbolism

(NOTE: These are some suggestions for topics; feel free to add to or delete from this list.)

Students within the group should prepare to "teach" their topic as it relates to *A Separate Peace*. Students should explain the role of each of these topics in the novel. They should find relevant passages and come to some reasonable conclusions about their topic as it relates to the book. One student in the group should be appointed secretary/spokesperson to write down and report the group's ideas.

Activity #3

Call students to your desk (or some other private area) to discuss their papers from Writing Assignment #2. A Writing Evaluation Form is included with this unit to help structure your conferences. Tell students when their revisions will be due. (Keep in mind that you need them for an activity in Lesson Fourteen.)

LESSON TWELVE

Objectives
1. To complete the group activity from Lesson Eleven
2. To allow students time to review, compare and correct their notes

Activity

Call on the groups to report the information they were able to compile. Jot the main points down briefly for students to copy into their notes. Use this as a springboard to discuss each of the topics.

LESSON THIRTEEN

Objective:

To discuss *A Separate Peace* on interpretive and critical levels

Activity #1

Choose the questions from the Extra Discussion Questions/Writing Assignments which seem most appropriate for your students. A class discussion of these questions is most effective if students have been given the opportunity to formulate answers to the questions prior to the discussion. To this end, you may either have all the students formulate answers to all the questions, divide your class into groups and assign one or more questions to each group, or you could assign one question to each student in your class. The option you choose will make a difference in the amount of class time needed for this activity.

Activity #2

After students have had ample time to formulate answers to the questions, begin your class discussion of the questions and the ideas presented by the questions. Be sure students take notes during the discussion so they have information to study for the unit test.

EXTRA WRITING ASSIGNMENTS/DISCUSSION QUESTIONS - *A Separate Peace*

<u>Interpretation</u>

1. Explain how John Knowles' using grown-up Gene as the narrator affects our understanding of the events in *A Separate Peace*.

2. What are the main conflicts in the story and how are they resolved?

3. Where is the climax of the story? Justify your answer.

4. Explain the importance of the setting in *A Separate Peace*

5. If you were to rewrite *A Separate Peace* as a play, where would you start and end each act? Explain why.

6. What opinions of his years at school does Gene have fifteen years later?

<u>Critical</u>

7. Describe Gene's relationship with Phineas.

8. Are Gene's actions believably motivated? Explain why or why not.

9. Compare and contrast Phineas and Gene.

10. Characterize John Knowles' style of writing. How does it contribute to the value of the novel?

11. Phineas and Gene were often said to be "a part of" each other. Explain what that means.

12. ". . . it seemed appropriate that my baptism there [in Naguamsett River] had taken place on the first day of this winter session, and that I had been thrown into it in the middle of a fight." Why did Gene think that was appropriate?

13. Explain the symbolic use of skiing, particularly the appropriate passages in Chapters 7 and 9.

14. Explain how the title relates to the events of the novel and the themes of *A Separate Peace*.

15. Explain Brinker's role in the novel. Why was he included?

16. Discuss the analogy of war sweeping over "like a wave at the seashore" in chapter 8.

A Separate Peace Extra Discussion Questions page 2

17. Are the characters in *A Separate Peace* stereotypes? If so, explain why John Knowles used stereotypes. If not, explain how the characters merit individuality.

18. Finny said, ". . . the whole world is on a Funny farm now. But it's only the fat old men who get the joke." What did he mean?

19. Leper said, "I'm almost glad this war came along. It's like a test, isn't it, and only the things and the people who've been evolving the right way survive." What is finally ironic about his thought?

20. What did Leper mean when he called Gene a "savage underneath"?

21. What views of the war did Gene, Finny, Brinker's father, Mr. Ludsbury have?

22. Why did Gene bounce on the tree limb causing Phineas to fall off?

23. Discuss the importance of the name "Super Suicide Society of the Summer Session," and the irony of the fact that Phineas thought of it.

Critical/Personal Response
24. Did Finny have to die to develop the themes of the novel? What effect did his death have, and how would the story have been different had he lived?

25. Were Finny and Leper both war casualties?

26. Brinker and Gene had two different ways of dealing with Finny's disability. Which was best? Why?

27. Who is responsible for Phineas' death?

28. Should Gene have been punished for his actions? By whom? What punishment?

29. Discuss the importance and the role of Cliff Quackenbush and Leper Lepellier in *A Separate Peace*.

Personal Response
30. Did you enjoy reading *A Separate Peace*? Why or why not?

31. What aspect of the story was most interesting to you?

32. Have you ever read another story with ideas or events similar to this one?

LESSON FOURTEEN

Objectives
1. To choose the editorials to be published in the newspaper
2. To give students the opportunity to practice writing to persuade
3. To give the teacher a chance to evaluate students' individual writing
4. To give students the opportunity to be creative

Activity #1

Divide your class into groups of four or five students. Give each group four or five of the editorials to evaluate. Be sure to take student names off of the papers so the judging will be impartial. Try not to give any group the papers for any of its group members.

Each student should read one composition orally to the remainder of the group. After all the compositions have been read, students should rank the compositions best (1), second-best (2), third-best (3), fourth-best (4) and fifth place (5). Judgement should be based on the relevance of the topic to *A Separate Peace*, how clearly the point of the editorial was made and how well the editorial was written. The rank should be written on the papers.

Activity #2

Collect all of the papers ranked 1. In the event that you have more than one editorial on the same topic, read the choices to the class and have the class vote as to which editorial is better for publication. If all the compositions cover the same topic, vote on which one should be used. Then, collect all of the papers ranked 2. Go through the same process. Ask then if anyone has compositions about topics other than those covered so far. If so, collect those and repeat the process. In the end, you should have at least a half a dozen editorials for your publication.

Activity #3

Distribute Writing Assignment #3. Discuss the directions in detail and give students ample time to complete it.

NOTE: These assignments will go through the same process as writing assignments 1&2. There will be writing conferences, students should make the revisions, the revisions will be ranked, and the class will vote on which ones should be published.

NOTE: Distribute the daily newspapers you have been using. When you read through the PROMPT section of the assignment sheet, stop and look at some of the advertisements in the newspaper with your class. Point out the common characteristics of the ads. (Grab the reader's attention, make the most important information stand out in the ad, make sure everything the reader needs to know is in the ad, etc.)

WRITING ASSIGNMENT #3 - *A Separate Peace*

PROMPT

Technologically advanced printing presses that print newspapers cost millions of dollars. Reporters, editors, layout people, pressmen, artists, and everyone associated with the newspaper production and delivery have to be paid salaries. Your daily newspaper which probably costs around fifty to seventy-five cents should cost at lest ten times that to cover the production costs. How, then, does the newspaper stay in business?

Advertising. They sell space in the newspaper to businesses and others who want to get product or other information to the people in your community. The cost of the advertising depends primarily on the size of the ad and the circulation (number of copies of the paper which will be printed and distributed). Ads in newspapers that reach tens of thousands or millions of people cost more than ads in little local papers that may only reach hundreds or a few thousand people.

If you own a retail business and purchase a full page ad in a paper that will reach tens of thousands of people, you will pay thousands of dollars. If you are spending that kind of money, you want the ad to be effective; that is, you want to make as many sales as possible from that ad. How do you do that?

Look now in the newspapers you have been using. Find examples of advertisements and create a list of characteristics they all have in common, a list of things that make a good ad.

Through advertisements, businesses and others try to persuade the public. You all will not be writing advertisements as your profession when you enter the workplace, but it is important for you to know how ads are constructed so as a consumer you can be aware of how you are constantly being manipulated by advertisements in newspapers, magazines, television, phone solicitations, and so on.

ASSIGNMENT

Your assignment is to create ONE of the following ads:
1. An advertisement for the winter carnival
2. An advertisement to get members to join the Super Suicide Society
3. An advertisement for Devon School
4. An advertisement for students to try out for the Olympics
5. An advertisement recruiting young men to the armed forces (choose the branch of service you wish or make it a general advertisement for all the armed forces)
6. An advertisement persuading people to support the war efforts

Since color advertising is about twice as expensive as black and white and our newspaper will be printed in black and white, your ads, likewise, must be done in black and white. They should be "camera ready," that is, they should be able to be printed "as is" without any corrections.

-

Separate Peace Writing Assignment #3 Page 2

PREWRITING

Stop and think about each of the topics, and see what kinds of ideas pop into your head. You'll probably have more or better ideas about one topic than all the rest. That's the topic you should choose.

Jot down your ideas on a piece of paper. Play with some sketches of your ideas to see which one seems to work the best. Choose the one that works best.

DRAFTING

Make a list of all the information you need to put into your ad. Keep revising your sketches until you have all the information you need in the ad placed in a way that conforms to the characteristics of a good ad. (Remember the list you made?)

PROMPT

When you finish the rough draft of your paper, ask a student who sits near you to read it. After reading your rough draft, he/she should tell you what he/she liked best about your work, which parts were difficult to understand, and ways in which your work could be improved. Reread your ad considering your critic's comments and make the corrections you think are necessary.

PROOFREADING

Do a final proofreading of your ad double-checking your spelling. Make a final copy of your ad suitable for publication.

LESSON FIFTEEN

Objectives:
1. To review the ads from Writing Assignment #3 and choose which ones will be published
2. To gather and organize all the articles to be published in the newspaper
3. To determine exactly how the newspaper will be published
4. To complete the newspaper project

NOTE: You need to decide how this newspaper will be published. Will you actually make it, put it together, and give each student a copy? Or will you have students make it? If students make it, who will you get to do it? Will you offer an extra-credit grade, exempt that/those student(s) from another activity, or what? Will you give it to your journalism class to put together? Perhaps a student who is taking a computer or word processing course would put it together. You know which options are most suitable for you, your class, and your school. Choose whichever is best, and let students know what will be done. This unit assumes you do the actual production of the newspaper outside of the regular class time.

Activity #1
Collect the ads from Writing Assignment #3. Using the opaque projector (if you have one--or just holding up the ads if you do not have a projector), show students each of the ads. Delete the students' names from the ads so judgement will be impartial. Discuss the good and bad points about each ad. Have students decide which of the ads are the best and are suitable for publication. Try to get one ad from each of the different topics advertised.

Activity #2
Explain to students that you now have enough materials to make your newspaper. Discuss a little bit about layout and design of a newspaper. Use the newspapers you have been using all along to show students what you mean by "column layout." Explain that the most important stories are put toward the front of the paper or to the front of each section of the paper. That is, the most important hard news stories are put on the front of the newspaper. The most important feature stories are put on the front of the feature section; the most important sports stories are put on the front of the sports section, and so on. Have students locate the editorial section of the papers.

Activity #3
Now that students know a little about the layout of a newspaper, have them decide where and in what order the materials you have gathered for your newspaper will go. Rank the hard news stories from most to least important. Rank the editorials from most to least important. The advertisements will be put in wherever they will fit.

If you decided to add feature story and/or sports story writing and the obituary (suggested in the Extra Activities section of this unit plan) have students rank the feature stories and sports stories from most to least important. Have students find the obituary column in the newspaper to see how the obituaries are done.

Activity #4

Now that students have done a basic, rough layout of the paper, tell them how the paper will be produced and when they might expect to see a copy of it.

LESSON SIXTEEN

Objectives
    1. To introduce the class project
    2. To give students the opportunity to work on their ads and to help students who are having trouble with their ads

Activity #1

Give students about fifteen minutes to work on their advertisements. Walk around the room to inspect the students' work and help students who may be having trouble.

Activity #2

Distribute the Class Project Assignment. Discuss the directions in detail.

NOTES TO THE TEACHER

1. READ THROUGH THIS ASSIGNMENT THOROUGHLY BEFORE INTRODUCING IT TO YOUR CLASS. If your students won't be able to handle it, or if it is against any school or local polices, DON'T DO IT.

2. This project is only intended to give students a "real" project in which they can practice their communications skills: thinking, organizing, persuading, informing, expressing personal opinions, etc. The introductory pages on the assignment sheet are intended to motivate students to put their best efforts into the project, nothing more.

3. So many communities are in need of help these days, and there are many students who would volunteer to do things if they only knew what to do. Inviting local leaders to talk with students opens the communications so school and community, parents, teachers and students can all work together for a safe, productive community.

4. BE SURE TO DISCUSS THIS ASSIGNMENT WITH YOUR ADMINISTRATION BEFORE UNDERTAKING IT.

CLASS PROJECT ASSIGNMENT - *A Separate Peace*
A Celebration of the American Spirit

PROMPT

The boys at Devon faced the immediate prospects of being personally involved in World War II. How about you? How much do you know about World War II? Maybe not much more than the boys from Devon. Have you studied about it in history class? Perhaps your attitude is, "Who cares about World War II, anyway? It is a dusty, old war that happened decades before I was born. So what?!"

Let's blow away the dust and take a fresh look at it from a different angle. The allied victory in World War II was a celebration of what was and is best in America. Think about it for a minute.

Why were we fighting? We fought for freedom and democracy, and we fought against tyranny and prejudice. What did the allies accomplish? We defeated Hitler and Mussolini and turned back the invading forces of Japan. We beat back the weeds of tyranny and prejudice so that individual people and nations could grow and flourish according to their own needs and desires. We advanced technology and changed the face of war forever. Americans joined together and pooled their ingenuity, resources and talents for one common purpose, and the results were fantastic.

It is with this in mind that we prepare a Celebration of the American Spirit in conjunction with the reading of *A Separate Peace* because of the influences of World War II in the novel.

PREPARATION

Before you begin planning your celebration, you need to define and understand what you are celebrating. That makes sense, right? What *is* the American Spirit? Make notes here:

YES, BUT WHAT HAVE YOU DONE FOR ME LATELY?

Like the students at Devon, you also have a war to fight; a war that, like World War II, has many battle fronts. You will have to fight the war on drugs, the war on crime, the wars on AIDS and cancer, and the war on the breakdown of the family and of our society. Some of you are out there on the battlefield already--you've been drafted, dragged into the war willing or not.

You and the people in your neighborhoods are the soldiers. Teachers, social workers, leaders of neighborhood associations--these are the lieutenants and colonels. The problem is that we are lacking generals and lacking the total commitment of the American Spirit that we had in WWII. Right now we're fighting skirmishes--a little battle here, a little battle there just trying to hold off the enemy rather than attacking with a full-scale offensive. I'm sure many of you feel like it's "every man for himself." The battle is real. Everyday in newspapers across the country, people read about people being shot, knifed, killed. People go "section 8" like Leper did or become very real members of the "suicide society."

What is our American Spirit? Where is it? Write your answer here:

A Separate Peace
American Spirit Celebration Assignment Page 2

GETTING BACK ON TRACK

What will be the spark that rekindles the American Spirit so it will again burn in the heart of our country and be a beacon for that which is good and just and true; so it will burn out apathy and short-sightedness and indifference? Write your answers here:

THE FOURTH OF JULY

Be a spark. You. . . .Yes, you. It's absurd. But that's where it's at. Without a spark, there is no fire. Period. Imagine if each one of you would be a spark; we'd have a sparkler! Imagine if you ignited the rest of the school. We'd have a firecracker! Imagine if your school could ignite your community and your community could ignite another. We'd have the Fourth of July!

The point is that it is up to you to find the American Spirit to help fight the battles we face ahead, and it is up to you to pass that spirit along so we as a nation of Americans can win the "war" against the forces that are undermining our country.

**   *   *   *   *   *

Gene said, ". . . I lost part of myself to him then, and a soaring sense of freedom revealed that this must have been my purpose from the first: to become a part of Phineas." Maybe that's a pretty good analogy to what it means to be an American. Each one of us gives up a little part of ourselves to our country--to become a part of something greater than any one person could be individually. In World War II, it wasn't any one soldier's death or any one general's idea or any one person's contribution to the war effort that made the allies successful. It was the fact that everyone gave something for the common good; everyone made a contribution to the greater cause.

THE BOTTOM LINE

So what are you going to do? For this assignment, you are going to plan one day of activities for your school to Celebrate the American Spirit. You are going to light a spark. You are going to have a pep rally for America. After that one day, will the spark be tended and turned into a flame? That's up to you. This is your chance to start--to take pride in your school, your community, your state and your country and to do your part to help begin win the war that faces us all.

YEAH, RIGHT. SURE. (HUMPF)

"It ain't gonna work." "Man, the war's too big." "You're nuts." "You gotta be part of the problem 'cause you gotta be on drugs if you think this will work!"

You're right. Standing up in the school auditorium, listening to the school band play the national anthem, and waving a few flags isn't going to do it. We're talking commitment and involvement here. We're talking about a really BIG project. We're talking about taking a real step in the real world---and you are going to be responsible.

A Separate Peace
American Spirit Celebration Assignment Page 3

GOTTA HAVE IT!
Enthusiasm, ideas, organization, determination--these are the requirements for success with this project. Some of you are probably a little enthusiastic already, some of you probably have some ideas. Determination is going to be important as time goes on. You have to be committed to complete this project.

REQUIREMENTS
1. You must plan one day's worth of activities relating to The American Spirit for your whole school.
2. You must have the approval of the teacher for each activity (just to make sure you don't do anything illegal or inappropriate).
3. Each activity must have a complete Activity Plan filled out and a complete Project Plan, including the Activity Plans, must be submitted to your teacher for approval by the principal before anything is done beyond the planning stage.
4. Do not go beyond the planning stage until the Project Plan is approved. That means don't contact guest speakers, community leaders, or anyone outside of the school until your teacher tells you it is okay.

ORGANIZATION
1. You have to elect two people who will be co-chairpersons of the project. These two people will be responsible for coordinating the project and act as a liaison to other people in authority (teacher, principal, community leaders if they will be involved).
2. Find out how much time you have to use on your American Spirit Day (or Pep Rally For America, or whatever you want to call it). You need to structure your activities so that every student in the school is scheduled to be somewhere specific under a specific teacher's guidance during the day.
3. As a group, decide what projects, what events, what activities you want to do. You need to estimate how long each activity will take. After you decide what you want to do, divide the class into committees, one committee for each activity.
4. Each committee should elect a chairman who will coordinate the group's efforts and keep the project co-chairpersons posted about progress. Each person in the committee should have specific tasks to do to make sure the activity is properly planned and executed.

A Separate Peace
American Spirit Celebration Assignment Page 4

SUGGESTIONS
1. Structure your Spirit Day in sections of time that match your current schedule. (If your class periods are 50 minutes long, make your activities in chunks of 50 minutes.) The less disruptive your schedule is to the normal routine, the more likely your plan will be approved. Consider lunch schedules and planning periods for teachers in your schedule. Consider scheduling students to participate in the activities by grade level or some other criteria your school normally uses for scheduling assemblies, pep rallies, etc.
2. Make the activities fun but also educational, interesting, and meaningful so that students come away from each activity a little richer, a little better educated, a little more informed than they were before.
3. Make sure students understand the purpose of this American Spirit Day. The idea is to get people involved with your school, your neighborhoods, your community, your city, your state, your America. Your goals are to give students a strong feeling of patriotism by showing them the best things America has to offer, to explore the difficult issues that face each one of us today and to search for ways to combat the problems in our society.

IDEAS
1. Begin the day with the Pledge to the Flag and the singing of *The Star Spangled Banner* and *America*.
2. Make a multi-media presentation in which you show what is RIGHT with America--why we are still flooded with immigrants and what we have to offer that most other places in the world do not. Start with clips from the past starting with the American Revolution and hit the highlights of our nation's accomplishments up through the present day. If you have a small school, show your multi-media presentation to all students in your auditorium or assembly room at the beginning of the day. If you have a large school, you may have to schedule different groups to see the presentation throughout the day.
3. Invite panels of guest speakers--your mayor, county council members, your board of education members, leaders in your community--and schedule them to meet with groups of students (say one class at a time) to discuss the problems in your area and ways the community and school are or could be working together to help solve those problems.
4. Invite MADD or your local "Just Say No!" campaign coordinators to show students how they can help combat those two trouble spots.
5. Coordinate a variety show around the American Spirit theme using students from your school and people from your community.
6. Have _____-A-Thons (fill in the blank with the activity or activities of your choice) to help raise money to improve your community. Have a specific goal in mind. Be sure to ask for business sponsors as well as individuals.
7. Have some American Spirit trophies or certificates made up. Have games/events that relate to the theme of the day, and use these as awards.
8. Invite a representative from your police department to come give safety tips and to discuss ways the public can help them in their efforts.
9. Maybe one of your local businesses would donate bumper stickers that say "The American Spirit--Catch It!" or some other appropriate slogan.
10. Have each one of the clubs in your school decorate one hallway based on the American Spirit theme.
These are just some basic ideas. You all are creative and can come up with some great ideas of your own--things that interest you and make use of your talents.

PROJECT PLAN

PROPOSED PROJECT NAME _____

PROPOSED BY _____

DATE OF PROPOSAL _____

SUBMITTED TO _____

PURPOSE OF THE PROJECT _____
_____
_____
_____
_____

DESCRIPTION OF THE PROJECT _____
_____
_____
_____
_____
_____
_____
_____
_____
_____

PROPOSED SCHEDULE OF EVENTS
_____
_____
_____
_____
_____
_____
_____
_____
_____
_____
_____

Proposal, Page 2

ADDITIONAL INFORMATION _____

_____
_____
_____
_____
_____
_____
_____
_____
_____
_____
_____
_____

NOTE: Attached to this proposal is an Activity Plan for each of the activities we would like to have for this project.

DATE(S) REQUESTED FOR THIS PROJECT:
                        _____ OR
                        _____ OR
                        _____

Comments from the person to whom this proposal is submitted:

Approved _____ Denied _____ Need More Information _____

_____   _____
Signature   Date

ACTIVITY PLAN

NAME OF PROPOSED ACTIVITY _____

PROPOSED BY _____

DATE _____

PURPOSE OF PROPOSED ACTIVITY _____
_____
_____
_____

DESCRIPTION OF PROPOSED ACTIVITY _____
_____
_____
_____
_____
_____
_____
_____
_____
_____
_____
_____
_____
_____

MATERIALS NEEDED _____
_____
_____
_____

SOURCE(S) OF MATERIALS _____
_____
_____
_____
_____

The page(s) which follow contain a detailed, step-by-step description of
how the activity will be planned and executed.

LESSON SEVENTEEN

Objective
   To give students the opportunity to work on the American Spirit class project

Activity
   Now that students have had overnight to think about the class project, use this class period to elect the co-chairpeople, brainstorm ideas about what students would like to do for activities, set up the committees, and elect committee chairpeople.

LESSON EIGHTEEN

Objective:
   1. To give students the opportunity to do any research necessary for their American Spirit project
   2. To give students time to work on their projects

Activity #1
   Take students to the library so they can do any research they need for the American Spirit project. You might suggest that they would try to find out what is being done in their community (communities) to combat drugs, crime, and other local problems. They should read back issues of local newspapers. If you live in a large city, perhaps someone publishes a magazine that would have helpful information.

Activity #2
   If students do not need to do any research or if the research they need to do cannot be done in your school library, give students this class time to continue working on the projects. Perhaps you could have a few students go to the office (or wherever phones are available) and call your county commissioners' office or city hall to get information about what kinds of things are being done in your communities to combat local problems, etc.

LESSON NINETEEN

Objective
   To review the main ideas presented in *A Separate Peace*

Activity
   Choose one of the review games/activities and spend your class period as outlined there. Some materials for these activities are located in the Extra Activities section of this unit.

REVIEW GAMES/ACTIVITIES - *A Separate Peace*

1. Ask the class to make up a unit test for *A Separate Peace*. The test should have 4 sections: matching, true/false, short answer, and essay. Students may use 1/2 period to make the test and then swap papers and use the other 1/2 class period to take a test a classmate has devised. (open book) You may want to use the unit test included in this packet or take questions from the students' unit tests to formulate your own test.

2. Take 1/2 period for students to make up true and false questions (including the answers). Collect the papers and divide the class into two teams. Draw a big tic-tac-toe board on the chalk board. Make one team X and one team O. Ask questions to each side, giving each student one turn. If the question is answered correctly, that students' team's letter (X or O) is placed in the box. If the answer is incorrect, no mark is placed in the box. The object is to get three marks in a row like tic-tac-toe. You may want to keep track of the number of games won for each team.

3. Take 1/2 period for students to make up questions (true/false and short answer). Collect the questions. Divide the class into two teams. You'll alternate asking questions to individual members of teams A & B (like in a spelling bee). The question keeps going from A to B until it is correctly answered, then a new question is asked. A correct answer does not allow the team to get another question. Correct answers are +2 points; incorrect answers are -1 point.

4. Have students pair up and quiz each other from their study guides and class notes.

5. Give students *A Separate Peace* crossword puzzle to complete.

6. Divide your class into two teams. Use the *A Separate Peace* crossword words with their letters jumbled as a word list. Student 1 from Team A faces off against Student 1 from Team B. You write the first jumbled word on the board. The first student (1A or 1B) to unscramble the word wins the chance for his/her team to score points. If 1A wins the jumble, go to student 2A and give him/her a clue. He/she must give you the correct word which matches that clue. If he/she does, Team A scores a point, and you give student 3A a clue for which you expect another correct response. Continue giving Team A clues until some team member makes an incorrect response. An incorrect response sends the game back to the jumbled-word face off, this time with students 2A and 2B. Instead of repeating giving clues to the first few students of each team, continue with the student after the one who gave the last incorrect response on the team. For example, if Team B wins the jumbled-word face-off, and student 5B gave the last incorrect answer for Team B, you would start this round of clue questions with student 6B, and so on. The team with the most points wins!

UNIT TESTS

SHORT ANSWER UNIT TEST 1 - *A Separate Peace*

I. Matching/Identify

____ 1. Brinker   A. Author

____ 2. Devon   B. The river

____ 3. Fat Men   C. He fell out of the tree & broke his leg

____ 4. Gene   D. Made up the war

____ 5. Knowles   E. Summer Head Master

____ 6. Leper   F. Went AWOL; First to enlist

____ 7. Ludsbury   G. Substitute master

____ 8. Naguamsett   H. Crew manager of the rowing team

____ 9. Patchwithers   I. Didn't know the war was propaganda because he was thin

____ 10. Phineas   J. He said the accident was Gene's fault

____ 11. Prudhomme   K. Location/Name of the school

____ 12. Quackenbush   L. Narrator

II. Short Answer

1. What two sites did the narrator go back to see at Devon?

2. What was the Super Suicide Society of the Summer Session?

3. What was blitzball?

Separate Peace Short Answer Unit Test 1 Page 2

4. What two realizations did Gene have about his relationship with Phineas (prior to Phineas' accident)?

5. "If you broke the rules, then they broke you." What did Gene mean?

6. Why did Gene feel a sense of freedom when Phineas said, "Listen, pal, if I can't play sports, you're going to play them for me"?

7. What effect did Leper's enlistment have on the boys at Devon?

8. Brinker said, "What's the matter with our class anyway? It isn't even June yet and we've already got two men sidelined for the Duration." Who was he talking about? For the duration of what?

9. Contrast Brinker's view of Finny's disability with Gene's.

10. Gene told Phineas, "You wouldn't be any good in the war, even if nothing had happened to your leg." What did he mean?

A Separate Peace Answer Unit Test 1 Page 3

III. Composition

What is the point of *A Separate Peace*? When we read books, we usually come away from our reading experience a little richer, having given more thought to a particular aspect of life. What do you think John Knowles intended us to gain from reading his novel?

IV. Vocabulary

Listen to the vocabulary words and write them down. Go back later and fill in the correct definition for each word.

1.

2.

3.

4.

5.

6.

7.

8.

9.

10.

SHORT ANSWER UNIT TEST 2 - *A Separate Peace*

I. Matching

____ 1. Brinker   A. Made up the war

____ 2. Devon   B. Summer Head Master

____ 3. Fat Men   C. Went AWOL; First to enlist

____ 4. Gene   D. Narrator

____ 5. Knowles   E. The river

____ 6. Leper   F. He fell out of the tree & broke his leg

____ 7. Ludsbury   G. He said the accident was Gene's fault

____ 8. Naguamsett   H. Crew manager of the rowing team

____ 9. Patchwithers   I. Location/Name of the school

____ 10. Phineas   J. Substitute master

____ 11. Prudhomme   K. Didn't know the war was propaganda because he was thin

____ 12. Quackenbush   L. Author

II. Short Answer

1. Gene said, "I didn't need to feel any tremendous rush of gratitude towards Phineas." Why not?

2. What did the swimming record incident show about Phineas?

3. Why didn't Gene tell Phineas the truth (that he bounced on the limb and caused the fall) at the infirmary?

A Separate Peace Answer Unit Test 2 Page 2

4. Why did Gene leave the Butt Room without smoking a cigarette?

5. For what event did Finny want to train Gene? What was wrong with that plan?

6. How did Gene react to Leper's description of what happened to him?

7. Brinker said, "What's the matter with our class anyway? It isn't even June yet and we've already got two men sidelined for the Duration." Who was he talking about? For the duration of what?

8. How did Leper's illness affect Phineas?

9. Why didn't Gene do anything to help with Phineas after his second accident?

A Separate Peace Answer Unit Test 2 Page 3

III. Composition: Write at least one complete paragraph for each answer.

1. Explain how the title *A Separate Peace* is appropriate.

2. Choose one theme from the *A Separate Peace*, identify it, and explain how it applies to the novel.

3. Compare and contrast Phineas and Gene.

4. What were the conflicts in the story, and how was each resolved?

A Separate Peace Answer Unit Test 2 Page 4

III. Vocabulary

Listen to the vocabulary words and write them down. Go back later and fill in the correct definition for each word.

1.

2.

3.

4.

5.

6.

7.

8.

9.

10.

KEY: SHORT ANSWER UNIT TESTS - *A Separate Peace*

The short answer questions are taken directly from the study guides.
If you need to look up the answers, you will find them in the study guide section.

Answers to the composition questions will vary depending on your
class discussions and the level of your students.

For the vocabulary section of the test, choose ten of the
words from the vocabulary lists to read orally for your students.

The answers to the matching section of the test are below.

Answers to the matching section of the Advanced Short Answer Unit Test
are the same as for Short Answer Unit Test #2.

Test #1	Test #2
1. J	1. G
2. K	2. I
3. D	3. A
4. L	4. D
5. A	5. L
6. F	6. C
7. I	7. K
8. B	8. E
9. E	9. B
10. C	10. F
11. G	11. J
12. H	12. H

ADVANCED SHORT ANSWER UNIT TEST - *A Separate Peace*

I. Matching

____ 1. Brinker   A. Made up the war

____ 2. Devon   B. Summer Head Master

____ 3. Fat Men   C. Went AWOL; First to enlist

____ 4. Gene   D. Narrator

____ 5. Knowles   E. The river

____ 6. Leper   F. He fell out of the tree & broke his leg

____ 7. Ludsbury   G. He said the accident was Gene's fault

____ 8. Naguamsett   H. Crew manager of the rowing team

____ 9. Patchwithers   I. Location/Name of the school

____ 10. Phineas   J. Substitute master

____ 11. Prudhomme   K. Didn't know the war was propaganda because he was thin

____ 12. Quackenbush   L. Author

II. Short Answer
1. From what point of view is *A Separate Peace* told, and how does that affect our understanding of the story?

A Separate Peace Advanced Short Answer Unit Test Page 2

2. Explain the importance of the setting in *A Separate Peace*.

3. ". . . it seemed appropriate that my baptism there had taken place on the first day of this winter session, and that I had been thrown into it in the middle of a fight." Why did Gene think that was appropriate?

4. Finny said, ". . . the whole world is on a Funny Farm now. But it's only the fat old men who get the joke." What did he mean?

5. Did Phineas have to die to develop the themes of the novel? What effect did his death have on the themes?

6. Explain why Leper Lepellier was an important character in the novel.

A Separate Peace Advanced Short Answer Unit Test Page 3

III. Composition
    Choose at least three different views of war given in *A Separate Peace* and explain each.

A Separate Peace Advanced Short Answer Unit Test Page 4

IV. Vocabulary

Listen to the vocabulary words and write them down. Go back later and write a composition using all the vocabulary words. The composition must relate in some way to *A Separate Peace*.

MULTIPLE CHOICE UNIT TEST 1 - *A Separate Peace*

I. Matching

____ 1. Brinker   A. Author

____ 2. Devon   B. The river

____ 3. Fat Men   C. He fell out of the tree & broke his leg

____ 4. Gene   D. Made up the war

____ 5. Knowles   E. Summer Head Master

____ 6. Leper   F. Went AWOL; First to enlist

____ 7. Ludsbury   G. Substitute master

____ 8. Naguamsett   H. Crew manager of the rowing team

____ 9. Patchwithers   I. Didn't know the war was propaganda because he was thin

____ 10. Phineas   J. He said the accident was Gene's fault

____ 11. Prudhomme   K. Location/Name of the school

____ 12. Quackenbush   L. Narrator

II. Multiple Choice

1. What two sites did the narrator go back to Devon to see?
    A. He went back to see the Butt Room and the dormitory.
    B. He went back to see the First Academy Building and the tree.
    C. He went back to see the river and the gym.
    D. He went back to see the Fields Beyond and the Crew House.

2. Why was the Super Suicide Society of the Summer Session created?
    A. It was created to talk the underclassmen out of taking an early enlistment in the service.
    B. It was created to get the boys to take flying lessons.
    C. It was created to help some of the boys who were depressed about the war, their grades, and other personal problems.
    D. It was created to formalize the jumping out of the tree ritual.

A Separate Peace Multiple Choice Unit Test 1 Page 2

3. Gene said,"" I didn't need to feel any tremendous rush of gratitude towards Phineas." Why not?
    A. Phineas would never show any gratitude to Gene, so Gene did not want to show any either.
    B. Phineas had not done anything that Gene considered out of the ordinary.
    C. Gene figured he wouldn't have been there in the first place if Finny had not talked him into it.
    D. Gene and Phineas were such close friends that they did not need to express their feeling aloud to each other. They each knew what the other was thinking and feeling.

4. What two realizations did Gene have about his relationship with Phineas?
    A. Phineas was jealous of Gene's being the head of the class and had deliberately set out to wreck his studies.
    B. Phineas didn't really like Gene but was using him to get help with studying and to borrow his (Gene's) clothes.
    C. They were friends only because they had been put in the same room; they had nothing in common that would carry the friendship over after they graduated from Devon.
    D. Gene didn't really like Phineas but was much too insecure to stand up to him.

5. Why didn't Gene tell Phineas the truth at the infirmary?
    A. Gene was afraid he would get expelled.
    B. Gene didn't remember exactly what had happened.
    C. Dr. Stanpole came in before Gene could tell him.
    D. Phineas was asleep and Gene didn't want to wake him.

6. What was Phineas' reaction when Gene did confess?
    A. He laughed and said it was all a joke.
    B. At first he didn't want to believe it. Then he asked Gene to leave.
    C. He got hysterical, threw his crutches at Gene, and said he wouldn't speak to him again.
    D. He said he had suspected it all along and that he would somehow get even.

7. How did Gene feel when Phineas said, "Listen, pal, if I can't play sports, you're going to play them for me"?
    A. He felt forgiven and that he had found a way to make up for his meanness.
    B. He felt trapped like he would be Finny's slave for the whole year.
    C. He felt resentful and thought that Phineas should admit to his handicap and get on with life.
    D. He felt excited because he always wanted the opportunity to excel at sports.

A Separate Peace Multiple Choice Unit Test 1 Page 3

8. How did Gene react to Leper's description of what happened to him?
    A. Gene felt sorry for Leper. He offered to help any way he could.
    B. Gene didn't believe it. He thought Leper was playing a practical joke on all of them.
    C. Gene thought it was the ski troop's fault. He decided to help Leper file
      a formal complain against them. He also decided he would never enlist himself.
    D. Gene didn't want to hear it. He told Leper to shut up and then he ran
      away and left Leper alone.

9. Brinker said, "What's the matter with our class anyway? It isn't even June yet and we've
   already got two men sidelined for the duration." Who and what was he talking about?
    A. He was talking about Gene and Phineas and the upcoming Olympics.
    B. He was talking about Leper and Phil Latham, who had quit school early.
    C. He was talking about Phineas and Leper and their inability to fight in the war.
    D. He was talking about Quackenbush and Gene not working together on the crew team.

10. Which describes Brinker's and Gene's views of Finny's disability?
    A. They both thought the boys should tease Finny to help him face his disability and get
      on with his life.
    B. Gene thought they should help Finny face his disability, but Brinker thought they
      should ignore it and hope it would get better.
    C. They both thought everyone should pity Finny and offer to help him
      as much as possible.
    D. Brinker thought they should help him face his disability and get on with his life.
      Gene thought they should ignore it and hope it would get better.

11. What finally happened to Phineas?
    A. He was released from the hospital and resumed his studies.
    B. He died because bone marrow got into his blood stream and stopped his heart.
    C. His leg had to be amputated. He became so depressed that his parents
      sent him to a rest home in Boston for a few months.
    D. He recovered partial use of his leg, but ended his friendship with Gene.

12. Which of these was *NOT* a conflict in *A Separate Peace*?
    A. Man vs. man
    B. Man vs. nature
    C. Man vs. himself
    D. None of the above

A Separate Peace Multiple Choice Unit Test 1 Page 4

III. Composition

Suppose you were a student at school with Phineas and Gene. What would you have said to each one of them after the second accident? Write one paragraph telling what you would have said to Gene and one paragraph telling what you would have said to Phineas. Be complete and show off as much knowledge of the story as you can.

A Separate Peace Multiple Choice Unit Test 1 Page 5

IV. Vocabulary: Match the correct definitions to the words.

___ 1. Animosity	a. Come to an end

___ 2. Innately	b. Intoxicating

___ 3. Insinuations	c. Short statements of truth; adages

___ 4. Sinecure	d. Impossible to detect with ordinary senses

___ 5. Aphorisms	e. Implications

___ 6. Incongruity	f. Not corresponding in character or kind

___ 7. Reverie	g. Bitter hostility

___ 8. Spectral	h. Deep-rooted, often mutual, hatred

___ 9. Idiosyncratic	i. A deadly poison; cause of ruin

___ 10. Bane	j. Extraordinary; impressively great

___ 11. Opulent	k. Present but not developed or active

___ 12. Prodigious	l. Inborn; inherently

___ 13. Puttee	m. Lower leg covering

___ 14. Cacophony	n. Discordant sounds

___ 15. Imperceptibly	o. Daydreaming

___ 16. Inebriating	p. Ghostly

___ 17. Latent	q. Luxurious

___ 18. Enmity	r. Peculiar

___ 19. Culminate	s. A paid position requiring little work

___ 20. Cliches	t. Trite or overused expressions

MULTIPLE CHOICE UNIT TEST 2 - *A Separate Peace*

I. Matching

____ 1. Brinker   A. Made up the war

____ 2. Devon   B. Summer Head Master

____ 3. Fat Men   C. Went AWOL; First to enlist

____ 4. Gene   D. Narrator

____ 5. Knowles   E. The river

____ 6. Leper   F. He fell out of the tree & broke his leg

____ 7. Ludsbury   G. He said the accident was Gene's fault

____ 8. Naguamsett   H. Crew manager of the rowing team

____ 9. Patchwithers   I. Location/Name of the school

____ 10. Phineas   J. Substitute master

____ 11. Prudhomme   K. Didn't know the war was propaganda because he was thin

____ 12. Quackenbush   L. Author

II. Multiple Choice

1. What two sites did the narrator go back to Devon to see?
    A. He went back to see the Butt Room and the dormitory.
    B. He went back to see the river and the gym.
    C. He went back to see the First Academy Building and the tree.
    D. He went back to see the Fields Beyond and the Crew House.

2. Why was the Super Suicide Society of the Summer Session created?
    A. It was created to formalize the jumping out of the tree ritual.
    B. It was created to get the boys to take flying lessons.
    C. It was created to help some of the boys who were depressed about the war, their grades, and other personal problems.
    D. It was created to talk the underclassmen out of taking an early enlistment in the service.

A Separate Peace Multiple Choice Unit Test 2 Page 2

3. Gene said,"" I didn't need to feel any tremendous rush of gratitude towards Phineas." Why not?
    - A. Phineas would never show any gratitude to Gene, so Gene did not want to show any either.
    - B. Phineas had not done anything that Gene considered out of the ordinary.
    - C. Gene and Phineas were such close friends that they did not need to express their feelings aloud to each other. They each knew what the other was thinking and feeling.
    - D. Gene figured he wouldn't have been there in the first place if Finny had not talked him into it.

4. What two realizations did Gene have about his relationship with Phineas?
    - A. They were friends only because they had been put in the same room; they had nothing in common that would carry the friendship over after they graduated from Devon.
    - B. Phineas didn't really like Gene but was using him to get help with studying and to borrow his (Gene's) clothes,
    - C. Phineas was jealous of Gene's being the head of the class and had deliberately set out to wreck his studies.
    - D. Gene didn't really like Phineas but was much too insecure to stand up to him.

5. Why didn't Gene tell Phineas the truth at the infirmary?
    - A. Gene was afraid he would get expelled.
    - B. Gene didn't remember exactly what had happened.
    - C. Phineas was asleep and Gene didn't want to wake him.
    - D. Dr. Stanpole came in before Gene could tell him.

6. What was Phineas' reaction when Gene did confess?
    - A. At first he didn't want to believe it. Then he asked Gene to leave.
    - B. He laughed and said it was all a joke.
    - C. He got hysterical, threw his crutches at Gene, and said he wouldn't speak to him again.
    - D. He said he had suspected it all along and that he would somehow get even.

7. How did Gene feel when Phineas said, "Listen, pal, if I can't play sports, you're going to play them for me?
    - A. He felt resentful and thought that Phineas should admit to his handicap and get on with life.
    - B. He felt trapped like he would be Finny's slave for the whole year.
    - C. He felt forgiven and that he had found a way to make up for his meanness.
    - D. He felt excited because he always wanted the opportunity to excel at sports.

A Separate Peace Multiple Choice Unit Test 2 Page 3

8. How did Gene react to Leper's description of what happened to him?
    A. Gene didn't want to hear it. He told Leper to shut up and then he ran
       away and left Leper alone.
    B. Gene didn't believe it. He thought Leper was playing a practical joke on all of them.
    C. Gene thought it was the ski troop's fault. He decided to help Leper file
       a formal complain against them. He also decided he would never enlist himself.
    D. Gene felt sorry for Leper. He offered to help any way he could.

9. Brinker said, "What's the matter with our class anyway? It isn't even June yet and we've
   already got two men sidelined for the duration." Who and what was he talking about?
    A. He was talking about Gene and Phineas and the upcoming Olympics.
    B. He was talking about Phineas and Leper and their inability to fight in the war.
    C. He was talking about Leper and Phil Latham, who had quit school early.
    D. He was talking about Quackenbush and Gene not working together on the crew team.

10. Which describes Brinker's and Gene's views of Finny's disability?
    A. They both thought the boys should tease Finny to help him face his disability and get
       on with his life.
    B. Gene thought they should help Finny face his disability, but Brinker thought they
       should ignore it and hope it would get better.
    C. Brinker thought they should to help him face his disability and get on with his life.
       Gene thought they should ignore it and hope it would get better.
    D. They both thought everyone should pity Finny and offer to help him
       as much as possible.

11. What finally happened to Phineas?
    A. He died because bone marrow got into his blood stream and stopped his heart.
    B. He was released from the hospital and resumed his studies.
    C. His leg had to be amputated. He became so depressed that his parents
       sent him to a rest home in Boston for a few months.
    D. He recovered partial use of his leg, but ended his friendship with Gene.

12. Which of these was NOT a conflict in *A Separate Peace*?
    A. Man vs. man
    B. Man vs. nature
    C. Man vs. himself
    D. None of the above

A Separate Peace Multiple Choice Unit Test 2 Page 4

III. Composition

About *A Separate Peace,* Aubrey Menen said, ". . . The characters are real, the tragedy is inevitable, the setting is perfectly chosen." Justify this statement.

A Separate Peace Multiple Choice Unit Test 2 Page 5

IV. Vocabulary - Match the definitions to the words.

___ 1. Idiosyncratic   a. Bitingly sarcastic or bitingly painful

___ 2. Latent   b. Trite or overused expressions

___ 3. Rhetorical   c. Short statements of truth; adages

___ 4. Curtly   d. Present but not developed or active

___ 5. Culminate   e. To go over extensively in the mind; ponder

___ 6. Mordantly   f. Not corresponding in character or kind

___ 7. Opulent   g. Come to an end

___ 8. Prodigious   h. Ashamed or uneasy

___ 9. Enmity   i. Luxurious

___ 10. Aphorisms   j. Bitter hostility

___ 11. Cliches   k. Deep-rooted, often mutual, hatred

___ 12. Zestfully   l. Concerned primarily with show or effect

___ 13. Infinitesimal   m. To get used to something undesirable

___ 14. Primevally   n. Extraordinary; impressively great

___ 15. Inebriating   o. Rudely brief; abruptly

___ 16. Mull   p. Intoxicating

___ 17. Abashed   q. Peculiar

___ 18. Inured   r. Immeasurably small

___ 19. Incongruity   s. With spirit or energy

___ 20. Animosity   t. Belonging to the earliest ages; ancient

ANSWER SHEET - *A Separate Peace*
Multiple Choice Unit Tests

I. Matching	II. Multiple Choice	IV. Vocabulary
1. ___	1. ___	1. ___
2. ___	2. ___	2. ___
3. ___	3. ___	3. ___
4. ___	4. ___	4. ___
5. ___	5. ___	5. ___
6. ___	6. ___	6. ___
7. ___	7. ___	7. ___
8. ___	8. ___	8. ___
9. ___	9. ___	9. ___
10. ___	10. ___	10. ___
11. ___	11. ___	11. ___
12. ___	12. ___	12. ___
13. ___	13. ___	13. ___
14. ___	14. ___	14. ___
15. ___		15. ___
16. ___		16. ___
17. ___		17. ___
		18. ___
		19. ___
		20. ___

ANSWER KEY - *A Separate Peace*
Multiple Choice Unit Tests

Answers to test 1 are in the left column. Answers to test 2 are in the right column.

I. Matching		II. Multiple Choice		IV. Vocabulary	
1. J	G	1. B	D	1. G	Q
2. K	I	2. D	A	2. L	D
3. D	A	3. C	D	3. E	L
4. L	D	4. A	C	4. S	O
5. A	L	5. C	D	5. C	G
6. F	C	6. B	A	6. F	A
7. I	K	7. A	C	7. O	I
8. B	E	8. D	A	8. P	N
9. E	B	9. C	B	9. R	K
10. C	F	10. D	C	10. I	C
11. G	J	11. B	A	11. Q	B
12. H	H	12. D	D	12. J	S
				13. M	R
				14. N	T
				15. D	P
				16. B	E
				17. K	H
				18. H	M
				19. A	F
				20. T	J

UNIT RESOURCE MATERIALS

BULLETIN BOARD IDEAS - *A Separate Peace*

1. Save one corner of the board for the best of students' *A Separate Peace* writing assignments.

2. Take one of the word search puzzles from the extra activities section and with a marker copy it over in a large size on the bulletin board. Write the clue words to find to one side. Invite students prior to and after class to find the words and circle them on the bulletin board.

3. Write several of the most significant quotations from the book onto the board on brightly colored paper.

4. Make a bulletin board listing the vocabulary words for this unit. As you complete sections of the novel and discuss the vocabulary for each section, write the definitions on the bulletin board. (If your board is one students face frequently, it will help them learn the words.)

5. Make a bulletin board about World War II. You could gather the materials yourself, or you could ask each student to bring in an article, pictures -- anything that could be stapled to the bulletin board--relating to World War II. Have your background paper up and title the board: A SEPARATE PEACE--STILL INFLUENCED BY THE WAR or some other appropriate title. Have each student explain what he/she has brought for the board, and post their articles.

6. Make a World War II bulletin board with a time line of the major events and battles. Perhaps a world map with allied countries marked in the same colors would be a good illustration. See a history teacher; perhaps he/she would have some good materials.

7. Title the board: YOUTH: A SEPARATE PEACE. Put up pictures of students doing activities. You could personalize this by putting up pictures of students in your school. (The yearbook or newspaper staff might be a good source of pictures. Or you could have students each bring in a picture of themselves and their friends doing something.)

8. If you are in an Olympic year, you could do a bulletin board about the Olympics. History of the Olympics would be especially appropriate. For example, on colorful paper write out interesting or noteworthy things related to the Olympics that have happened throughout the years. Put up lots of pictures to add color and visual interest.

9. Make a World War II bulletin board. Put up background paper. Have each student take a marker and write up one fact he/she knows about World War II. If you have a small class, you could go around the class two or three times.

EXTRA ACTIVITIES

One of the difficulties in teaching a novel is that all students don't read at the same speed. One student who likes to read may take the book home and finish it in a day or two. Sometimes a few students finish the in-class assignments early. The problem, then, is finding suitable extra activities for students.

The best thing I've found is to keep a little library in the classroom. For this unit on *A Separate Peace,* you might check out from the school library other related books and articles about World War II, life in America in the 1940's, the Olympics, dealing with jealousy in friendships, or sports. Articles written about *A Separate Peace* would be good to have on hand. Also, information about and other books by the author would be of interest to some students.

Other things you may keep on hand are puzzles. We have made some relating directly to *A Separate Peace* for you. Feel free to duplicate them.

Some students may like to draw. You might devise a contest or allow some extra-credit grade for students who draw characters or scenes from *A Separate Peace*. Note, too, that if the students do not want to keep their drawings you may pick up some extra bulletin board materials this way. If you have a contest and you supply the prize (a CD or something like that perhaps), you could, possibly, make the drawing itself a non-refundable entry fee.

The pages which follow contain games, puzzles and worksheets. The keys, when appropriate, immediately follow the puzzle or worksheet. There are two main groups of activities: one group for the unit; that is, generally relating to the *Separate Peace* text, and another group of activities related strictly to the *Separate Peace* vocabulary.

Directions for these games, puzzles and worksheets are self-explanatory. The object here is to provide you with extra materials you may use in any way you choose.

MORE ACTIVITIES - *A Separate Peace*

1. Pick a chapter or scene with a great deal of dialogue and have the students act it out on a stage. (Perhaps you could assign various scenes to different groups of students so more than one scene could be acted and more students could participate.)

2. Have students make a model of Devon School or draw a map of the campus. Students should use as many details from the novel as possible and fill in plausible information where the specific information is lacking in the novel.

3. Have your students plan a Winter Carnival for your school.

4. Have students design a book cover (front and back and inside flaps) for *A Separate Peace*.

5. Have students design a bulletin board (ready to be put up; not just sketched) for *A Separate Peace*.

6. Rewrite the ending of the story as a group writing activity. Basically you would pick a point from which the story should be rewritten, then students (considering the characters, themes, author's style, etc.) would offer suggestions as to how it could be rewritten. Make an outline and then have students actually give the sentences as they think they should appear (including dialogue, etc.). It is one way to have students do a creative writing assignment and use all of the skills involved without your having to grade *another* stack of papers.

7. Have a 1940's day. Students could research different aspects of the 1940's and give oral reports in the costume of the day, with your room decorated appropriately. You can make this as simple or as involved as you want!

8. Discuss *A Separate Peace* from the angle that people do need a way or a place to "get away from it all" occasionally--a way or a place to get away from the stresses of everyday life. Discuss ways people do this and suggest ways students (and grownups!) can relax, de-stress, and generally relieve their minds of troublesome things. Perhaps have a psychologist come in as a guest speaker to discuss this topic with your students.

9. Discuss war with your students--what it means to be at war or to go to war, how it affects not only those in the military, but everyone in a country. Talk about the wars and conflicts that are going on in the world today. Discuss how students would feel if they had to go to war, or if a war were going on in our country the way it is in other countries.

10. Discuss the causes of wars and how leaders manipulate the people of their countries to get them to fight their battles. Use specific examples from history.

WORD SEARCH - *A Separate Peace*

All words in this list are associated with *A Separate Peace*. The words are placed backwards, forward, diagonally, up and down. The included words are listed below the word searches.

```
G K V A G B L A K C G H E L X L P Q Z B R K J T
J J X W W K R S C S O N W G L Y S H X S G W R W
S M S N G O D E K C L N F A R Z S W I R O E B Z
S C I P M Y L O K I I D F A C T S F I N N Y L T
K Y H C O O F N S N P D W E A F E D S M E L G M
L Y H O D O O T Y D I G E I S S F L G T A A Q G
G E N E O W R R S R W R R N R S U T E B R N S K
T Z P Z L L A T T E N S B E T U T I Z G O E R J
D D G E W M R L R T E P H Y C E L T C V R E E F
B B S Z R O A C W Z U T M L S O I E E I D A E J
V Q W I P V S Y I L I B F M U L R D S U D T M Z
L J F S I U M G E W F D A A B D J D T S A E C D
S N V N O E O V H K H U Q Q T D S I T R C N G V
I S R L D L O C C M G H F K V M T B A T H H F M
H A A A O H T L M A R R O W M A E P U Q C L H R
C E C P S A Z Y N C P S K T R M E N C R Q V K V
J A A Z P R U D H O M M E G Y S L S F V Y P H C
```

ACADEMY	ENLIST	LUDSBURY	SKI
ACCIDENT	FACTS	MARROW	SNOW
APOLOGIZE	FALL	NAGUAMSETT	SPORTS
AWOL	FATMEN	OLYMPICS	STAIRS
BLITZBALL	FINNY	PATCHWITHERS	SUICIDE
BRINKER	GENE	PHINEAS	SWIM
BUTTROOM	GRATITUDE	PRUDHOMME	TELEGRAM
CARNIVAL	INFIRMARY	RECORD	TREE
CHET	JEALOUS	RULES	TROOPS
CONFESS	KNOWLES	SCHOOL	WAR
CREW	LEG	SEPARATE	DEVON
LEPER	SHOVEL		

CROSSWORD - *A Separate Peace*

CROSSWORD CLUES - *A Separate Peace*

ACROSS

1. Phineas wanted to organize a Winter _____
4. Devon _____
10. Narrator
11. Gene went to the infirmary to _____ to Phineas
13. Gene caused Phineas to ___ out of the tree
15. Phineas could no longer play ___ after the accident.
16. Wait a ----; sixty seconds
18. Phineas fell out of it because Gene bounced on the limb
19. Join the army
20. Didn't know the war was propaganda because he was thin
24. Scene of Gene's first mock trial; smoking room
26. Snow removal hand tool
27. Location of the school
29. Phineas said that they made up the war
30. ____ jump; planned winter carnival activity
31. They rode on the train; those who had enlisted
36. Short sleep
37. He said Gene bounced Finny out of the tree on purpose
39. Gene thought Phineas was ___ of his being head of the class.
41. Big event going on in the world at the time of the story
42. Stern, summer Head Master
44. Holler; speak loudly
45. Put food in one's body
46. Phineas liked to do this water activity
47. The First ____ Building

DOWN

1. Winter Carnival trumpeter
2. If you broke the ___, then they broke you.
3. Leper went this to avoid a Section Eight discharge
5. Rowing team members for one boat
6. Finny wanted to train Gene for the 1944 _____.
7. Phineas broke his
8. Admit to doing something
9. Nickname for Phineas
10. I didn't need to feel any tremendous rush of ___ towards Phineas
11. Not on purpose; by _____
12. Scene of Finny's second fall
14. First to enlist; he went AWOL
17. Substitute Master
21. Past tense of 'bleed'
22. The river
23. Doctor's office/ sick room at the school
24. Game Phineas invented in which all the players are enemies
25. One rows with these
28. Brinker wanted all the ___ out in the open
30. A _____ Peace
32. Possess
33. The boys cleared this from the railroad tracks.
34. Author
35. It got into Phineas' blood stream and stopped his heart
38. Phineas wanted to break the swimming _____.
40. Halt
43. Passing fancy

CROSSWORD ANSWER KEY - *A Separate Peace*

				C	A	R	N	I	V	A	L			S	C	H	O	O	L	
				H		U			W		C		F		R		L		E	
		G	E	N	E		L		A	P	O	L	O	G	I	Z	E		G	
		R		T			E		C		L		N		N		W		M		S
F	A	L	L				S		C				F		N			S	P	O	R	T	S
		T		E				M	I	N	U	T	E		Y		P			A
		I		P					D				S				R		C			I
		T	R	E	E				E	N	L	I	S	T		L	U	D	S	B	U	R	Y
		U		R					N								D		L		S			N
		D			I		B	U	T	T	R	O	O	M		S	H	O	V	E	L			A
D	E	V	O	N		L				A			F			O		D					G
				F		I				R		F	A	T	M	E	N						U
		S	K	I		T	R	O	O	P	S		C		M					S		A
K		E		R		Z		W					T		E				M		N		M
N	A	P		M		B	R	I	N	K	E	R		S			J	E	A	L	O	U	S
O		A		A		A						E				S		E		W		E
W	A	R		R		L			P	A	T	C	H	W	I	T	H	E	R	S		T
L	A			Y	E	L	L				O		H			O				O			T
E	A	T									R		I		P		S	W	I	M			T
S		E				A	C	A	D	E	M	Y											

MATCHING QUIZ/WORKSHEET 1 - *A Separate Peace*

___ 1. FINNY　　　　　　　A. Didn't know the war was propaganda because he was thin

___ 2. MARROW　　　　　　B. Phineas said that they made up the war

___ 3. PATCHWITHERS　　　C. Narrator

___ 4. SWIM　　　　　　　D. The river

___ 5. FALL　　　　　　　E. Phineas broke his

___ 6. CONFESS　　　　　　F. Phineas could no longer play ___ after the accident.

___ 7. FATMEN　　　　　　G. They rode on the train; those who had enlisted

___ 8. ACCIDENT　　　　　H. Phineas wanted to break the swimming _____

___ 9. GENE　　　　　　　I. It got into Phineas' blood stream and stopped his heart

___ 10. ACADEMY　　　　　J. Brinker wanted all the ___ out in the open

___ 11. ENLIST　　　　　　K. Doctor's office/ sick room at the school

___ 12. LEG　　　　　　　L. Winter Carnival trumpeter

___ 13. LUDSBURY　　　　　M. Admit to doing something

___ 14. FACTS　　　　　　N. Nickname for Phineas

___ 15. SPORTS　　　　　　O. The First ____ Building

___ 16. NAGUAMSETT　　　　P. Join the army

___ 17. TROOPS　　　　　　Q. Phineas liked to do this water activity

___ 18. CHET　　　　　　　R. Stern, summer Head Master

___ 19. INFIRMARY　　　　S. Gene caused Phineas to ___ out of the tree

___ 20. RECORD　　　　　　T. Not on purpose; by accident

MATCHING QUIZ/WORKSHEET 2 - *A Separate Peace*

___ 1. FALL   A. It got into Phineas' blood stream and stopped his heart

___ 2. FATMEN   B. Doctor's office/ sick room at the school

___ 3. FINNY   C. Finny wanted to train Gene for the 1944 _____.

___ 4. LEG   D. Brinker wanted all the ___ out in the open

___ 5. FACTS   E. Gene caused Phineas to ___ out of the tree

___ 6. CHET   F. Nickname for Phineas

___ 7. RECORD   G. Phineas broke his

___ 8. TREE   H. Game Phineas invented in which all the players are enemies

___ 9. MARROW   I. Phineas wanted to break the swimming _____

___ 10. PHINEAS   J. Didn't know the war was propaganda because he was thin

___ 11. WAR   K. Big event going on in the world at the time of the story

___ 12. OLYMPICS   L. Narrator

___ 13. INFIRMARY   M. They rode on the train; those who had enlisted

___ 14. ACCIDENT   N. Stern, summer Head Master

___ 15. BLITZBALL   O. Winter Carnival trumpeter

___ 16. LUDSBURY   P. Not on purpose; by accident

___ 17. TROOPS   Q. Scene of Finny's second fall

___ 18. GENE   R. Phineas fell out of it because Gene bounced on the limb

___ 19. PATCHWITHERS   S. Gene's best friend and roommate

___ 20. STAIRS   T. Phineas said that they made up the war

KEY: MATCHING QUIZ/WORKSHEETS - *A Separate Peace*

Worksheet 1	Worksheet 2
1. N	1. E
2. I	2. T
3. R	3. F
4. Q	4. G
5. S	5. D
6. M	6. O
7. B	7. I
8. T	8. R
9. C	9. A
10. O	10. S
11. P	11. K
12. E	12. C
13. A	13. B
14. J	14. P
15. F	15. H
16. D	16. J
17. G	17. M
18. L	18. L
19. K	19. N
20. H	20. Q

JUGGLE LETTER REVIEW GAME CLUE SHEET - *A Separate Peace*

SCRAMBLED	WORD	CLUE
DROCER	RECORD	Phineas wanted to break the swimming _____.
RWA	WAR	Big event going on in the world at the time of the story
DISECIU	SUICIDE	The Super _____ Society of the Summer Session
ALLF	FALL	Gene caused Phineas to ____ out of the tree
EKSOWLN	KNOWLES	Author
TSRAEEAP	SEPARATE	A _____ Peace
EGL	LEG	Phineas broke his
TISSAR	STAIRS	Scene of Finny's second fall
YDMCAAE	ACADEMY	The First _____ Building
OSWN	SNOW	The boys cleared this from the railroad tracks
SCAFT	FACTS	Brinker wanted all the _____ out in the open
OTPSOR	TROOPS	They rode on the train; those who had enlisted
UGAEMSATNT	NAGUAMSETT	The river
NNFYI	FINNY	Nickname for Phineas
MIWS	SWIM	Phineas liked to do this water activity
TGIUDRTEA	GRATITUDE	I didn't need to feel any tremendous rush of _____ towards Phineas
DMHOURPEM	PRUDHOMME	Substitute Master
REWC	CREW	Rowing team members for one boat
ALCRAIVN	CARNIVAL	Phineas wanted to organize a Winter _____
KENRRIB	BRINKER	He said Gene bounced Finny out of the tree on purpose
LISTEN	ENLIST	Join the army
EIASNHP	PHINEAS	Gene's best friend and roommate
AFRNMIIYR	INFIRMARY	Doctor's office/sick room at the school
ECTH	CHET	Winter Carnival trumpeter
AOJSULE	JEALOUS	Gene thought Phineas was ____ of his being head of the class
KIERBNR	BRINKER	He said Gene bounced Finny out of the tree on purpose
TEATCSHHIRWP	PATCHWITHERS	Stern, summer Head Master
NTEDACIC	ACCIDENT	Not on purpose; by accident
ROSTSP	SPORTS	Phineas could no longer play ____ after the accident
TOTUOBMR	BUTTROOM	Scene of Gene's first mock trial; smoking room
ERLPE	LEPER	First to enlist; he went AWOL
LOAW	AWOL	Leper went this to avoid a Section Eight discharge

ORMAWR	MARROW	It got into Phineas' blood stream and stopped his heart
YLURUSBD	LUDSBURY	Didn't know the war was propaganda because he was thin
RWA	WAR	Big event going on in the world at the time of the story
OSLOCH	SCHOOL	Devon _____
EAIGOOPLZ	APOLOGIZE	Gene went to the infirmary to _____ to Phineas
ISK	SKI	_____ jump; planned winter carnival activity

VOCABULARY RESOURCE MATERIALS

VOCABULARY WORD SEARCH - *A Separate Peace*

All words in this list are associated with *A Separate Peace* with an emphasis on the vocabulary words chosen for study in the text. The words are placed backwards, forward, diagonally, up and down. The included words are listed below.

```
C W B E R G L C R T C I J I L D X Y L R D R J V
Y U T I C N Z Q I V W A N A G N L V Q Q N Z L Q
T T L N N N J C L T V N C U N T Z Q R Y M Z V M
P R I M E V A L L Y A P H O R I S M S M L A U Q
Q R U M I T E N A T L R I U P E M I J X T L W J
L L O C N N C I E B I T C N L H D O N W M P T K
L W N D O E A L G T A N N N E A O P S E B S P K
B A N E I N Y T I L S S A A Y B T N U I C B K B
Z C C C D G T L E C E U H N D S R E Y T T U H J
R Q D I A T I E L G H D S E E R O I N H T Y R L
X E F L R P H O N U H E O D D N O I A T K E D E
V R V T D O A L U T F G S P R G S M D T V G E B
K Z Z E R L T C M S I T C T U F P X L I I R T P
B J Y R R T C E I P G O S G S L S T X M M N M L
D B R Q M I M R H O Y Z U E T P E R P Z S K G K
D V K H X P E B Q R U D G S Z G F N R Z R J T W
M K J D L F Z T R H Z S Z J S P E C T R A L Z K
```

ABASHED	CULMINATE	INVEIGLED	QUALMS
ANIMOSITY	CURTLY	LATENT	REVERIE
APHORISMS	ENMITY	MORDANTLY	RHETORICAL
BANE	IDIOSYNCRATIC	MULL	SINECURE
CACOPHONY	INANE	OPULENT	SPECTRAL
CAPACIOUS	INEBRIATING	PRIMEVALLY	SUSTENANCE
CLICHES	INNATELY	PRODIGIOUS	TACIT
CONTENTIOUS	INURED	PUTTEE	ZESTFULLY

VOCABULARY CROSSWORD - *A Separate Peace*

VOCABULARY CROSSWORD CLUES - *A Separate Peace*

ACROSS
2. Rudely brief; abruptly
5. Luxurious
10. To go over extensively in the mind; ponder
11. You put it on a hurt part of your body to keep swelling down
12. Not spoken
14. Bitingly sarcastic or bitingly painful
16. Phineas broke his
17. Throw; threw; have -----
18. The boys were ---- from the war draft because they were in school
19. Narrator
20. Wager
21. ____ jump; planned winter carnival activity
24. Rowing team members for one boat
27. Spacious; roomy
28. Phineas fell out of it because Gene bounced on the limb
30. If you broke the ___, then they broke you.
32. Where the war was; out of one's own country
33. Bitter hostility
34. Shove
39. Ashamed or uneasy
40. Inborn; inherently
43. The Super _____ Society of the Summer Session
44. You use one to row a boat
45. Nice; easy to get along with; agreeable
47. Possess
48. Partner to 'that'
50. A paid position requiring little work
51. Give way to
53. The boys cleared this from the railroad racks.
54. One who lies
55. Head, legs, arms, abdomen are parts of a ----
56. There are 100 of these on a football field

DOWN
1. Impossible to detect with ordinary senses
2. Trite or overused expressions
3. Concerned primarily with show or effect
4. Present but not developed or active
6. Lower leg covering
7. Deep-rooted, often mutual, hatred
8. Lacking in sense or substance
9. Come to an end
13. Winter Carnival trumpeter
15. Daydreaming
22. Gene caused Phineas to ___ out of the tree
23. Doubts
25. Big event going on in the world at the time of the story
26. Location of the school
29. Implications
31. Devon _____
33. Short statements of truth; adages
35. A deadly poison; cause of ruin
36. Discordant sounds
37. With spirit or energy
38. He said Gene bounced Finny out of the tree on purpose
41. The First ____ Building
42. Nickname for Phineas
43. Snow removal hand tool
46. First to enlist; he went AWOL
49. Leper went this to avoid a Section Eight discharge
52. Gene and Phineas were one; a pair; two together

VOCABULARY CROSSWORD ANSWER KEY - *A Separate Peace*

	I		C	U	R	T	L	Y		O	P	U	L	E	N	T		I			C	
	M	U	L	L		H		A				U		N				N			U	
	P		I	C	E		T	A	C	I	T			M	O	R	D	A	N	T	L	Y
L	E	G		C		T		E		H		T		I		E		N			M	
	R		T	H	R	O	W	N		E	X	E	M	P	T		V		E		I	
	C		E		R		T		T		E			Y		E				G	E	N	E
B	E	T		S	K	I			F				Q			C	R	E	W		A	
	P		D			C	A	P	A	C	I	O	U	S			I		A		T	
	T	R	E	E		A			L			A		I		E		R	I	L	E	S
	I		V			L			L			L		N								C
A	B	R	O	A	D				A	N	I	M	O	S	I	T	Y		P	U	S	H
	L		N			B		C		P		S		I				Z				O
	Y			B	A	B	A	S	H	E	D		I	N	N	A	T	E	L	Y		O
		F		R		N		C		O				U		C		S				L
S	U	I	C	I	D	E		O	A	R		P	L	E	A	S	A	N	T			
H		N		N			P		I					T		D		F		L		
O	W	N		K		T	H	I	S		A		S	I	N	E	C	U	R	E		
V		Y	I	E	L	D		O	M		W			O		M		L		P		
E				R	U	N		S	N	O	W			N		Y		L		E		
L	I	A	R		B	O	D	Y			L			S				Y	A	R	D	S

VOCABULARY WORKSHEET 1 - *A Separate Peace*

___ 1. Extraordinary; impressively great
    a. Qualms   b. Curtly   c. Prodigious   d. Innately

___ 2. Quarrelsome; not getting along
    a. Qualms   b. Opulent   c. Contentious   d. Idiosyncratic

___ 3. Spacious; roomy
    a. Capacious   b. Culminate   c. Incongruity   d. Qualms

___ 4. Belonging to the earliest ages; ancient
    a. Mull   b. Culminate   c. Puttee   d. Primevally

___ 5. Inborn; inherently
    a. Bane   b. Innately   c. Sustenance   d. Preeminently

___ 6. Lower leg covering
    a. Contentious   b. Puttee   c. Cacophony   d. Mull

___ 7. Not corresponding in character or kind
    a. Reverie   b. Spectral   c. Cliches   d. Incongruity

___ 8. Coaxed
    a. Mull   b. Aphorisms   c. Inveigled   d. Inebriating

___ 9. Outstandingly
    a. Cacophony   b. Culminate   c. Puttee   d. Preeminently

___ 10. Discordant sounds
    a. Zestfully   b. Rhetorical   c. Insinuations   d. Cacophony

___ 11. Ghostly
    a. Contentious   b. Spectral   c. Rhetorical   d. Culminate

___ 12. Come to an end
    a. Culminate   b. Contentious   c. Imperceptibly   d. Mull

___ 13. Not spoken
    a. Culminate   b. Spectral   c. Contentious   d. Tacit

___ 14. Luxurious
    a. Sustenance   b. Mull   c. Sinecure   d. Opulent

___ 15. Implications
    a. Innately   b. Insinuations   c. Capacious   d. Sustenance

___ 16. With spirit or energy
    a. Curtly   b. Sinecure   c. Zestfully   d. Mull

___ 17. Doubts
    a. Capacious   b. Qualms   c. Bane   d. Animosity

___ 18. Ashamed or uneasy
    a. Innately   b. Aphorisms   c. Incongruity   d. Abashed

___ 19. A deadly poison; cause of ruin
    a. Contentious   b. Bane   c. Incongruity   d. Infinitesimal

___ 20. Bitingly sarcastic or bitingly painful
    a. Mordantly   b. Opulent   c. Zestfully   d. Mull

VOCABULARY WORKSHEET 2 - *A Separate Peace*

___ 1. IDIOSYNCRATIC   A. Bitingly sarcastic or bitingly painful

___ 2. LATENT   B. Trite or overused expressions

___ 3. RHETORICAL   C. Short statements of truth; adages

___ 4. CURTLY   D. Present but not developed or active

___ 5. CULMINATE   E. To go over extensively in the mind; ponder

___ 6. MORDANTLY   F. Not corresponding in character or kind

___ 7. OPULENT   G. Come to an end

___ 8. PRODIGIOUS   H. Ashamed or uneasy

___ 9. ENMITY   I. Luxurious

___ 10. APHORISMS   J. Bitter hostility

___ 11. CLICHES   K. Deep-rooted, often mutual, hatred

___ 12. ZESTFULLY   L. Concerned primarily with show or effect

___ 13. INFINITESIMAL   M. To get used to something undesirable

___ 14. PRIMEVALLY   N. Extraordinary; impressively great

___ 15. INEBRIATING   O. Rudely brief; abruptly

___ 16. MULL   P. Intoxicating

___ 17. ABASHED   Q. Peculiar

___ 18. INURED   R. Immeasurably small

___ 19. INCONGRUITY   S. With spirit or energy

___ 20. ANIMOSITY   T. Belonging to the earliest ages; ancient

KEY: VOCABULARY WORKSHEETS - *A Separate Peace*

Worksheet 1	Worksheet 2
1. C	1. Q
2. C	2. D
3. A	3. L
4. D	4. O
5. B	5. G
6. B	6. A
7. D	7. I
8. C	8. N
9. D	9. K
10. D	10. C
11. B	11. B
12. A	12. S
13. D	13. R
14. D	14. T
15. B	15. P
16. C	16. E
17. B	17. H
18. D	18. M
19. B	19. F
20. A	20. J

VOCABULARY JUGGLE LETTER REVIEW GAME CLUES - *A Separate Peace*

SCRAMBLED	WORD	CLUE
EONTPLU	OPULENT	Luxurious
YINTLEMNEPER	PREEMINENTLY	Outstandingly
TIYOINSAM	ANIMOSITY	Bitter hostility
IECCSLH	CLICHES	Trite or overused expressions
UMSQAL	QUALMS	Doubts
EINAN	INANE	Lacking in sense or substance
NIDURE	INURED	To get used to something undesirable
LMUL	MULL	To go over extensively in the mind; ponder
AICUCOASP	CAPACIOUS	Spacious; roomy
NGIIANIRTEB	INEBRIATING	Intoxicating
ODSPIRIGOU	PRODIGIOUS	Extraordinary; impressively great
LIITINNSAFEIM	INFINITESIMAL	Immeasurably small
ILMPVLRYEA	PRIMEVALLY	Belonging to the earliest ages; ancient
NEUATSCSEN	SUSTENANCE	Support for life
ITACT	TACIT	Not spoken
UFTSELLYZ	ZESTFULLY	With spirit or energy
IMSSAHROP	APHORISMS	Short statements of truth; adages
NETATL	LATENT	Present but not developed or active
RNOYDMATL	MORDANTLY	Bitingly sarcastic or bitingly painful
EREIREV	REVERIE	Daydreaming
SEDBAAH	ABASHED	Ashamed or uneasy
RIRCTOAELH	RHETORICAL	Concerning primarily with show or effect
CERINEUS	SINECUREA	Paid position requiring little work
OISIDCCINTYAR	IDIOSYNCRATIC	Peculiar
ENAB	BANE	A deadly poison; cause of ruin
USAIIOTNNNSI	INSINUATIONS	Implications
GDELVNIIE	INVEIGLED	Coaxed
HYPNCCOAO	CACOPHONY	Discordant sounds
LYCRUT	CURTLY	Rudely brief; abruptly
NATICELUM	CULMINATE	Come to an end
CEYIIPRBLTEPM	IMPERCEPTIBLY	Impossible to detect with ordinary senses
ANITNYEL	INNATELY	Inborn; inherently
YTENIM	ENMITY	Deep-rooted, often mutual, hatred